AEC LORRIES in the POST~WAR YEARS 1945~1979

GRAHAM EDGE

ROUNDOAK PUBLISHING, NYNEHEAD, WELLINGTON, SOMERSET

First published in 1994 by
Roundoak Publishing
Nynehead, Wellington, Somerset, England TA21 0BX.

© Copyright 1994 **Graham Edge & Roundoak Publishing**

ISBN 1 871565 21 9

Design and Typesetting by
Palatine Hill Limited
Yeovil, Somerset

Origination by
Colorhouse
Sherbourne, Dorset

Printed in Guernsey by
Guernsey Press Company Limited
Vale, Guernsey.

ACKNOWLEDGEMENTS

Such a book as this, about a subject as complex as AEC, could
not have been completed without the help, assistance, and
advice of many individuals. Harry Pick has been a most helpful
source, and has willingly shared his great knowledge of the
technical details of the vehicles. He has also given me valuable
insights into the company policies and objectives, and has
patiently and thoroughly checked my manuscript for factual
and technical errors, and suggested suitable amendments.
Brian Goulding has offered much advice and many helpful
suggestions about the text and layout.

Arthur Ingram has opened up his extensive
photographic collection to me, allowing me a free choice of his
photographs to use, including several official AEC ones which
were thought to have been lost, but thankfully are in Arthur's
care.

Group Captain Bill Taylor O.B.E. has taken many AEC
photographs, and in addition to allowing me to use some of
them, he has provided information about the AECs operated
by the RAF.

Judith Temple has transferred the manuscript onto her
word processor.

The following people have provided photographs and
information: Bevan Laing, Jack Henley, Peter Davies, Raymond
Jenkins (Motorphoto), J.Morris Bray, Mrs Joyce Harwood, Ken
Durston, Fernand Van De Plas (Belgium), F. Michel (France),
Gordon Baron, and Jim Wilkinson. Many others have also
contributed, often unknowingly, many years ago.

To them all I give my sincere thanks and appreciation,
and hope that they are satisfied with the results of my efforts.

Graham Edge,
Swaffham Prior, June 1994.

Front cover photograph

On an early spring day in 1966, a Mercury tractor unit and
single axle semi-trailer belonging to Hichens of Penzance,
negotiates a bend on an undulating road in south west
England. Powered by the AV505 engine and operating at 24
tons gross train weight when this photograph was taken, the
Mercury was the leading medium weight tractor unit of its era.
(AEC)

AEC LORRIES in the POST~WAR YEARS 1945~1979

INTRODUCTION

The Associated Equipment Company Ltd. was formed at Walthamstow on the 13th June 1912, and on 25th May 1979 the last vehicles whose ancestry could be traced back through the intervening years were completed at the Southall plant of what had become AEC Ltd. and then a part of the Leyland Group. The majority of the vehicles built firstly at Walthamstow, then at Southall carried the name 'AEC' and the organisation which built them had in general terms, for the purpose of this book, a life of 67 years. This is not a long time for a company to exist, but in that timespan AEC, as it was known for most of those years, achieved more, in terms of commercial vehicle innovation and development, than many organisations have achieved.

The origins of AEC pre-dated its registration in June 1912 by a few years, as it emerged from the repair workshops of two previously merged London bus companies, namely Vanguard and the London General Omnibus Company who had joined forces in 1907. The latter name abbreviated to LGOC was retained. In the early years of the twentieth century the hundreds of horse-drawn buses operating in London were being rapidly replaced by new motorised buses which were mainly of imported makes. The repair workshops of the LGOC for its motor buses were located at Walthamstow in east London and it was here that AEC was formed in 1912 to design and build new bus chassis which could also be offered for sale to customers other than the parent company. So, from the first days of its formation AEC was fortunate in having a huge potential market to fulfil as the LGOC and its competitors rapidly replaced their horse-drawn buses with motor buses.

Earlier in 1912 the LGOC had been taken over by the Underground Electric Train Company of London, and this situation existed until July 1933 when the London Passenger Transport Board was formed by the amalgamation of various

passenger carriers operating in the capital at that time. With the formation of this new body, AEC was floated on the Stock Exchange as a public company, although it was fortunate in retaining its favoured position as the major supplier of buses to the new organisation, an association which was to last until the late 1960s.

The Great War of 1914-18 caused AEC to produce goods chassis for the first time, in quantities which at that time were unprecedented. To satisfy the demands of the armed forces over 10,000 'Y-Type' 3-4 tonners were built, and from then on goods and passenger chassis were built side by side. At the end of the first World War AEC started to establish its sales to customers other than its parent company. In those pioneering days of motorised transport, development was so rapid that a certain model might only have a production life of a couple of years or so before being rendered obsolete by its successor. AEC were innovative in many ways, not least in their assembly methods, and a moving track was installed at Walthamstow. When the decision was made to build a completely new factory on a 63 acre green field site at Southall on the then western outskirts of London, the moving track was taken from Walthamstow and installed at Southall in 1926. The Walthamstow factory was completely vacated by AEC with the local

labour force being bused to Southall daily for many years.

It is true to say that for most of its existence AEC was an engineer led company. That is not to say that its products were purely functional, as is often the case in such instances: the vehicles were always well finished with many attractive designs through the years. This engineering expertise showed itself in the design of the vehicle components and the proven engineering principles applied. The detailed finish extended to the nickel plating of controls and many component parts, even cylinder head nuts: stove enamelling of such items as valve rocker covers as well as chrome plating of front wheel nut cover rings: and later, rear hub covers with enamelled AEC logos. All pointers to a high quality of build and finish which set AEC vehicles apart from their competitors.

The AEC after-sales service was legendary for its efficiency for all of its life. Each regional AEC depot had an area Service Engineer who always liaised closely with all customers, however large or small, to iron out any problems with vehicles in service. Every chassis was despatched with a strong wooden packing case securely banded to it, which contained a large tool roll in which was a 1½ lb hammer, chisel, large, medium and small screwdrivers, a set of open ended spanners, (sizes ¼" BSF – 1⅛" BSF), and a wheelbrace and jack. There was also a white card for the owner to complete when the vehicle entered service, and on receipt of this card at Southall a workshop manual would be then forwarded.

Like many other commercial vehicle builders in the late 1920s AEC investigated and developed the high speed diesel engine for automotive applications. Some companies evolved their early designs from slow speed marine units, but AEC adapted a clean sheet approach and in 1928 they had their own prototype engine running in one of the works transport buses. The 'Oil Engine', as it was then known, was developed by C.B. Dicksee at AEC and in 1930 the first production oil engine was offered to customers. This was an 8.1 litre unit of 95 bhp. By 1934 this had been developed into an 8.8 litre unit producing up to 130 bhp at 2400 rpm, both very high figures for the time. Two four cylinder oil engines of 5.3 litres and 6.61 litres capacities were also introduced at this time. AEC had worked along with the Ricardo Engineering Consultancy Company and the A165 8.8 litre engine utilised the AEC-Ricardo Comet cylinder head and combustion chamber design with indirect fuel injection.

AEC were always willing to co-operate with other companies: in the 1920s there was a partial merger with Daimler, and soon after World War 2, there was a joint trolley bus building venture with Leyland well before the two companies merged. Maybe AEC persisted with indirect fuel injection on their oil engine for rather too long, probably influenced by London Transport who were striving for a smooth and quiet oil engine to replace petrol engines. When the direct fuel injection version of the A173 7.7 litre engine was introduced in 1937 it was to become their standard engine for many years, eventually setting standards for economy, reliability and longevity.

AEC were the first to build an internal combustion engined rigid 8 wheeler in 1934. There had been steam powered examples built before then, and a few of the first Mammoth Major eights to be built were petrol engined. The names Mammoth Major and AEC became synonymous, and it was appropriate that when the last true AEC goods vehicle chassis was built at Southall in mid 1977, it was indeed a Mammoth Major eight.

AEC always favoured the completely integrated building philosophy, that is, designing and building all the main chassis components themselves. That did not stop them agreeing to customer demands, and some early diesel engined chassis were fitted with Gardner engines from new. Many petrol engined chassis were re-engined in later years as the economies of the diesel engine gained acceptance, and again, Gardner engines were sometimes used in such cases.

In the tilt-cab era, the Fuller nine speed range change gearbox was an optional fitting in Mandator and Mammoth Major chassis. AEC were always very willing suppliers of their engines and gearboxes to other vehicle builders both at home and overseas with Albion, Atkinson, Dennis, Dodge, ERF, Guy, Maudslay, Rowe-Hillmaster, and Seddon using engines, and sometimes gearboxes, in this country, and Vanajan in Finland and Willeme in France doing likewise.

Over the years the engine range was developed in size and power output, and in each class of vehicle AEC always at least matched, and usually bettered, the power outputs of their competitors. In addition to road-going applications AEC also supplied engines for many and various industrial and marine uses, including railcars. As well as moving, a vehicle has to stop and AEC were always very aware of this fact. For many years AEC had easily the best brakes in the business with air pressure brakes being standard on the heavy chassis range from Mk III onwards. When introduced in 1953 the Mercury medium weight had vacuum assisted hydraulic brakes, but when the Mk II Mercury was announced a couple of years later, it too had full air pressure brakes, unprecedented at the time for a medium weight chassis. In fact such was the reputation of AEC brakes in the days when many large hauliers built their own drawbar and semi-trailers, they would use the trailing rear axles from old multi-axle AEC chassis for their trailers, because the braking performance was superior to anything else. Passenger vehicle developments often overlapped into the goods vehicle range with AECs always appearing to be sympathetically sprung, and giving a comfortable ride for the driver and his load.

As the business grew AEC absorbed Maudslay and Crossley in 1948, both highly respected vehicle builders, with Maudslay particularly having a golden heritage of engineering expertise.

This aerial photograph of the Southall site was taken in 1962, when AEC celebrated its Golden Jubilee. In the foreground is the then newly constructed chassis inspection shop, fronting onto Windmill Lane. The building in the top left hand front corner is the service department, with the main machine shops, engine building plant, and assembly lines at the far end of the site. Unusually for such a large manufacturer, AEC never operated their own foundry, with all castings being sourced from outside suppliers. Because of local planning restrictions imposed on the large expanse of sports fields, any further expansion was prohibited, so to all intents and purposes the 63 acre site was full at this date. (*AEC*)

During the 1950s Maudslay became the axle building facility for the Associated Commercial Vehicles Group as it was by then called as well as building non-standard Mk III chassis, fire engine chassis for Merryweather, the new Mercury chassis, and the Mustang twin steer 6 wheeler. They also developed and built the massive 18 cu.yd. Dumptruk which was powered by a huge 17.89 litre AEC engine. The takeover of the bodybuilders, Park Royal Vehicles also affected the goods vehicle range, with many Mk III, Mk V and Mercurys being fitted with cabs built at Park Royal.

In 1961 Thornycroft, another long established and respected company, came into the ACV Group. Their own goods vehicle range was quickly phased out in favour of AEC models, but they handled other specialist vehicle developments and produced gearboxes for the group.

From the days of the first World War and the building of the 'Y-Type' for the armed forces, AEC enjoyed a good relationship with the Government's procurement agencies, and steady orders for military vehicles were obtained for many years. The Matador 4 x 4 Artillery Tractor achieved a legendary status during the Second World War, and many of these ubiquitous vehicles are still hard at work 50 years after being built.

The Militant range in both 6 x 4 and 6 x 6 format was supplied to the Army in large numbers, and to the RAF from the early 1950s until the early 1970s, and aircraft refuelling bowsers were being supplied to the Royal Navy and the RAF from 1940 until the early 1970s. In addition to these specialist vehicles many civilian models were used by all branches of the armed forces for transport duties.

At the time of writing, AEC vehicles are still operated by the Army and RAF, and it can be said that AECs have participated in every armed conflict this century involving British forces where motorised transport has been required. This includes more recent actions such as the Falklands Invasion and the Gulf War.

Another characteristic of AEC was the tremendous loyalty it enjoyed from customers. Once AECs were bought by a customer he usually bought more of them for many years. Several well known large transport fleets in Great Britain were entirely AEC. Many operators stayed loyal right until the end with vehicles continuing to work well beyond their expected life. It was significant that when the AEC range was discontinued these operators did not purchase corresponding Leyland models, but switched their allegiance to other marques, usually of foreign origin.

This marque loyalty to AEC extended overseas as they built a world wide business with thousands of chassis exported. The main overseas markets were in the former British Empire, but overall in excess of sixty countries had some AEC representation. Surprisingly several in South America were staunch AEC operators,

and some vehicles are still in service there to this day, principally in Uraguay and Argentina. AECs were badged ACLO for this market to avoid confusion with the German AEG electrical goods company. Portugal also became a large user of AEC buses and lorries and continued to import chassis until 1979.

With the tremendous benefit of hindsight the demise and closure of AEC should never have been allowed to happen, and that statement applies to all of the once great and proud British commercial vehicle industry. Sadly, in this country we seem only to appreciate something when it no longer exists. The merger in 1962 of Leyland Motors and the ACV Group should have led to great things for the new company. Both Leyland and AEC had established growing and prosperous export markets and the idea behind the merger was to consolidate these markets.

The Government inspired takeover in 1968 of the massive car and light commercial vehicle makers BMC, which was in desperate trouble, made the new enlarged group unwieldy and virtually unmanageable. The huge financial losses being incurred by the car making divisions in the group starved the still (at that time), profitable heavy goods vehicles divisions of the necessary development and investment funds. Coupled with poor management, baffling decisions, differences of opinion between top people at Leyland and Southall, and political interference from Whitehall, the group was in no position to combat the growing imports of all types of vehicle into Great Britain. It all proved to be too much, and if a foreign agency had deliberately set out to sabotage our heavy vehicle building industry they could not have done a better job! The export markets were quickly lost and the ailing monster created with such initial optimism gradually died a death of a thousand cuts.

Fifteen years after Southall closed it is still possible to feel anger and frustration about it all. No product is ever perfect and some particular AEC models did have a few problems over the years, but they had fewer problems than other contemporary makes, and they were profitable trucks to operate and good trucks to drive. Anyone who was driving or starting a driving career between the years 1945-80 probably drove an AEC at some time. Operators and drivers still remember them with respect, and, yes, affection, and seldom have a bad word to say about them.

This book about AEC trucks during the years since 1945 is not intended to be a purely technical, or definitive treatise about AECs, but it is hoped that it will outline the development of the marque and give a representative view of the vehicles and their operations in the conditions pertaining to road transport at the time. Hopefully it will re-kindle a few fond memories of one of our greatest makes of truck. Whenever possible the photographs have been selected to depict the vehicle in a working situation, rather than specifically posed 'Motorshow' publicity type shots.

CHAPTER ONE

THE IMMEDIATE POST~WAR YEARS 1945~1947

When war was declared on 3rd September 1939, at a moments notice the AEC Southall factory was declared a 'Protected Place' and became subject to the Official Secrets Act. Very soon afterwards production of AEC goods and passenger chassis for civilian use came to an end, with all the production facilities being turned over to the war effort. Vehicles in the final stages of being built were completed and despatched to a few customers. It has been suggested that a very few Mammoth Major Mk II eight wheelers were built after 1940. This is true, and they along with a handful of Mammoth Minors were allocated under Ministry of War Transport permits to selected operators.

The wartime demands placed upon Southall were huge and AEC responded in magnificent fashion and met all of its production target deadlines despite difficulties in obtaining supplies of raw materials and skilled labour. During the war years over 5000 new employees were recruited, many of them to replace workers called up in the armed forces, and this alone required an intensive training programme. About one quarter of the workforce were women during these years. Many of the senior AEC designers and engineers were seconded to various Government Ministries and Departments and these posts were covered at Southall by bringing in staff from the AEC regional depots.

The AEC war effort has been well documented and

in total 12,896 military vehicles of all types were built. The majority of these were the famous 4 x 4 853/0853 Matador Medium Artillery Tractor, with 8,612 being completed in 2 axle format. A further 1,514 6 x 6 type 854/0854 models were built, mainly for the RAF as petrol bowsers, but some of these chassis were equipped with a Coles crane. The majority of the Matadors were powered by a modified version of the 7.7 litre diesel engine, designated as type A187. The early 6 x 6 vehicles, type 854, were powered by a 6 cylinder OHC petrol engine rated at 120 bhp, probably in the interests of a common fuel supply at the RAF stations where they operated. Later 6 x 6 vehicles, type 0854, were fitted with the standard A187 7.7 litre diesel engine. The third vehicle type built in quantity was another 4 x 4, an AEC – designed armoured car which evolved through three versions, with the final Mk III type being powered by the A197 9.6 litre diesel engine.

In addition to building these vehicles Southall produced tank suspension units and a large number of engines. For the Matilda tank Southall made 400 pairs of A183/4 6.6 litre diesel engines, which were 'handed' so they could drive through a common transmission; also for the Valentine tank, AEC produced 350 petrol engines and 3,250 A190 9.6 litre diesel engines.

In addition the AEC workers built a large number of 4 cylinder and 6 cylinder diesel stationary engines, which were used for a multitude of purposes, including generating sets for powering standby radar units and

searchlight batteries. Perhaps the most demanding and critical task was given to the AEC engines which provided all of the power for the spectacular Mulberry Harbours which were constructed to facilitate the landing of men, equipment and supplies in the days following the Normandy invasion in June 1944.

As the war progressed it was realised that there was a necessity for some vehicles for civilian purposes, particularly public transport. The Guy factory at Wolverhampton was designated to build buses equipped with a 'Utility' design of body powered by Gardner engines. In 1943 Daimler at Coventry also commenced building passenger chassis to receive the same 'Utility' bodies, using the standard AEC A173 7.7 litre diesel engine. Bristol was allowed to build passenger chassis and used an alternative 7.7 litre diesel engine, designed as a direct replacement for Gardner 5LW units and designated as type A202. Similarly, Maudslay built lorries during these years using the AEC A173 engine and the relatively young companies of ERF, founded in 1933, and Atkinson, re-formed also in 1933, were authorised to build lorries with AEC engines for allocation to civilian operators and contractors. ERF built mainly 2 axle rigids and tractor units using the A202 7.7 litre engine, and Atkinson built one hundred 3

axle, and one hundred 4 axle rigids, mainly for use as Pool Petroleum tankers. Again the A202 7.7 litre engine was the mainstay, although it has been written that some of the eight wheelers were fitted with the AEC 9.6 litre engine. Careful examination of the AEC sales records, and the Atkinson chassis build sheets for this period have failed to confirm this.

Notwithstanding all this war effort activity, existing civilian vehicles had to be kept on the roads, and the repair and overhaul facilities, not only at Southall, but also at the AEC regional depots, worked round the clock to keep them going.

When peace returned to a war weary nation in 1945 there was a pent up demand for all types of buses and lorries to replace vehicles which in many cases should have been withdrawn years earlier, but necessity had forced them to carry on operating through the war years. The supply of raw materials was still very difficult and the Ministry of Supply operated a permit system, not only for the allocation of new vehicles, but for all manner of goods, including steel. The Southall plant was faced with a multitude of problems in re-adjusting to peace time working practices. Fortunately the main production and assembly areas had escaped any serious bombing damage during the war, with just the Spares

Above left: Dating from the mid-1930s, Turners of Soham operated this Monarch (chassis no. 0647 021), until the late 1950s. It had previously been owned by A.E. Newport Ltd. of Fordham. The canvas flap on the side of the body was to allow easier loading of eggs at one of the packing stations where it was not possible to reverse up to the loading bank. (*Arthur Ingram*)

Above: The type 640 Mercury was produced from 1929-37, and many served for 20 years or more, as did this Trinidad Lake Asphalt compressor carrier. This company had a liking for normal control lorries, and they also used several bus chassis as tippers. *(Arthur Ingram)*

and Service department having been hit: but much of the machinery was worn out from the war effort and had at least to be overhauled, and in many instances, replaced. Those employees fortunate enough to return after anything up to six years in the forces had to learn again the different disciplines of civilian, as opposed to military life, and the traumatic experiences to which many had been subjected. The whole picture in the immediate post-war years was one of drab austerity, and the euphoria of victory quickly evaporated away with the stark realities of shortages and rationing.

Just as the nation and its people were weary, so were the vehicles. Apart from the 'Utility' buses and authorised lorries built during the war years, all types of civilian transport had to rely on vehicles which were at least 7 years old in 1946, and in most cases, much older than that. This situation was entirely different from that at the end of the 1914-18 Great War. Then, thousands of war surplus vehicles had been released for sale into civilian markets, often after re-building by their original manufacturer. Unlike then the majority of heavy vehicles built for the 1939-45 war were of a specialist type and were unsuitable for most civilian users. At the lighter end 'O' type Bedfords and such like did sterling service for years in civilian use, but at the heavier end of the

transport fleet very few former military vehicles were suitable, apart from some ERFs and Fodens.

Before the war AEC had developed its goods range into the heavy market. They did build a lightweight, the Mercury with a choice of petrol or diesel engines, but never established a large presence in this particular market as their main rival Leyland had done with the successful Cub and Lynx models.

In 1939 the main AEC goods vehicle range consisted of five 2 axle models, two 3 axle models, and one 4 axle model. The 'lightest vehicles were the Monarchs: type 344 was a forward control Mk I, and type 0244 was the bonneted normal control Mk II version. Both were powered by a choice of 4 cylinder diesel engines of either 5.3 or 6.61 litres which were an OHC design. Type 0346 was a forward control Monarch Mk II powered by the A173 7.7 litre diesel engine, and there were two versions of a Matador Mk II, which was a 4 x 2 vehicle and not to be confused with the 4 x 4 military vehicle. Type 0246 was the normal control vehicle, and type 0346 Matador was the forward control version similar to the type 0346 Monarch apart from the addition of a 2 speed auxiliary gearbox in the driveline to augment the standard 4 speed D124 gearbox. The Matador was equipped for drawbar trailer work, powered by the A173 7.7 litre engine. A choice of wheelbase lengths was available on all the 2 axle models for different applications. Tractor units for coupling to semi-trailers were not very popular because of stability and jack-knifing problems associated with articulation, which were not resolved until braking systems were re-designed in later years. The multi-axle models were the type 0366 Mammoth Major 6 Mk II, and the type 0386 Mammoth Major 8 Mk II, both powered by the A173 7.7 litre diesel engine, with drive through a 4 speed D124 main gearbox and two speed auxiliary gearbox to give a 'super top' and 'super bottom' ratio. Final drive was either a single drive bogie with spiral bevel double reduction axle, or double drive by overhead worm and wheel with third differential.

A Mammoth Minor, type 0366L was also available and was introduced to increase the payload of the type 0346 Monarch by the fitment of an unequally sprung, lightweight trailing single wheel third axle fitted with standard front axle hubs and brakes. Power was from the A173 7.7 litre engine with 4 speed D124 gearbox, but no auxiliary gearbox, resulting in mediocre performance when some operators actually fitted twin rear wheels and used their 'Minors' as 'Majors' at 19 tons gross vehicle weight. Many of these pre-war vehicles carried on in service into the 1950s and even 1960s as the post war demand for new goods vehicles was virtually insatiable.

When peace returned and normal production resumed at Southall much of the production capacity was given over to producing passenger vehicles for London Transport and other customers. The goods vehicles offered were based on the immediate pre-war Mk II, but there were some important changes. Decisions had been taken to standardise on two engine sizes, the by now well proven A173 7.7 litre diesel, and the A206 9.6 litre diesel which had been introduced in 1939. No petrol engine options were offered and the 4 cylinder Monarch was not re-introduced.

The evolution of these two standard engines had been an interesting feature of the pre-war years. The A173 7.7 litre diesel engine eventually became AECs first successful direct injection engine and its bore dimensions of 105mm and stroke of 146mm actually gave a capacity of 7,585 cc. When introduced in 1937 it had a new design of toroidal cavity piston which gave easy starting on the coldest of mornings without the need for pre-heating glow plugs. The AEC indirect fuel injection engines were notoriously bad starters, with burning oil-soaked rags often being held above air intakes to get them going. AEC had persisted with indirect fuel injection, mainly at the behest of London Transport who required a quiet diesel engine to replace their petrol engines and also to match the Leyland direct injection diesel engine which was noted for its quietness and smoothness. Also, diesel fuel quality standards were variable and filtration primitive, which could result in very small injector nozzles easily blocking up in direct injection engines.

The A173 engine had two cylinder heads covering three cylinders each, and a high-mounted cam shaft and short push rods. It was a simple and effective design. Originally the crankcases and sumps were made of aluminium alloy known as RR60 metal, but when the war started supplies of this metal were directed entirely to Rolls Royce for their aero engines, and AEC reverted to a cast iron crankcase. This actually improved the engine as it made it considerably more rigid and increased the main and big end bearing life by a considerable margin. A change of bearing metal also helped in this regard. Whilst the earlier A165 8.8 litre indirect injection diesel engine was a more powerful unit, the 7.7 litre engine had been designed to compete with the Gardner 5LW and 6LW engines which were popular choices with many bus operators. Like the Gardner engine, the AEC 7.7 litre design was a long

Above: A typical Monarch Mk II was this tilt bodied one, operated by Thomas Glover & Co. Ltd., manufacturers of 'Main' gas appliances. They also had a number of AEC Majestics; one of which survives in Norfolk. (Arthur Ingram)

post war Mammoth Majors it produced up to 125 bhp at 1,800 rpm.

The A173 7.7 litre engine was used in the immediate post war Monarch, designated as type 0346S, with the 'S' meaning for solo use. The 4 x 2 Matador, type 0347 was re-introduced for drawbar trailer work and again was powered by the A173 7.7 litre engine.

The model designation numbers of the Mammoth Majors became 0366/20 and 0386/20 for the six and eight wheelers respectively.

The standard pre-war Mk II chassis received the A206 9.6 litre engine with 4 speed D124 gearbox and 2 speed auxiliary gearbox. Braking performance was improved by fitting vacuum servos to the front axle brakes. Some chassis did receive a larger clutch and the new 5 speed constant mesh gearbox, together with a stronger rear differential for trailer work. The Mammoth Minor was not offered, and again no specialist heavy tractor unit was available. Various wheelbase lengths were available for all types, for different applications. AEC were purely chassis builders with cabs mainly being coach built affairs: maybe being built by the AEC dealer such as Oswald Tillotson and by large body builders such as Park Royal Vehicles (PRV) or Hampshire Car Bodies (HCB), but in many instances by the local body builder of the lorry operator. They were of a simple functional design offering the driver little in terms of comfort, warmth, or sound proofing, and their usual ash frame construction offered little or no protection in the event of a collision.

The Duramin company did build a lighter, alloy cab in the mid 1930s, in the interests of reducing the unladen weight of the vehicle. The London Brick Company were one of the first AEC operators to buy this cab as weight saving measures were always uppermost in their thoughts. At this time they were also using aluminium alloy in the construction of the load carrying platform body in place of traditional hard wood. With this type of cab and body, small radiator, 30 gallon fuel tank, and 36 x 8 tyres on lightweight wheels, the unladen weight of their 8 x 2 Mammoth Major Mk IIs

Above: Although badged as a Monarch, this Bristow's AEC is more likely to be a Matador Mk II, because of the short rear chassis overhang. The operators were one of the well remembered Davis Bros'. companies and it was photographed in Holloway Road, London, in the years when it was possible to stop a lorry at the roadside – before the advent of the 'red route'. (*Arthur Ingram*)

stroke unit, giving good low engine speed torque and pulling power. There had been an A171 7.7 litre indirect injection engine, but the piston and cylinder head design of the A173 7.7 litre engine was completely different from its predecessor. The two 4 cylinder engines had shared a common stroke of 146mm with the 7.7 litre engine, but were of a totally different OHC design with bores of 108mm (5.3 litre engine) and 120mm (6.61 litre engine) respectively. In its post war guise the A173 7.7 litre engine produced up to 105 bhp at 1.800 rpm.

The A165 8.8 litre indirect injection engine had evolved into the A180 direct injection engine by 1938, but London Transport had started to favour an even larger capacity engine, lightly stressed and of modest power output to give a longer operating life for its bus operations.

From this concept a new engine of 9.636 litres capacity, type A204, was designed to power the famous RT bus which was introduced in 1939. The bore was 120mm and the 142 stroke dimension of the 8.8 litre engine was retained, but unlike the old engine the crankcase was split at the centre line of the crankshaft. The water pump, fan and dynamo were belt driven as opposed to chain driven. It also had bolted down cylinder heads in original format, but this design gave rise to considerable problems in service with early examples, and new engine blocks with studs had to be substituted. Early engines also had cooling water circulation problems which could result in piston seizure, but the system was re-designed to circulate more water to the rear of the second cylinder head, so curing the problem. Once these problems had been resolved the A206 9.6 litre engine evolved into a thoroughly reliable and efficient unit, and as used in the

was 6 lbs below 6 tons, giving them a legal payload of 16 tons of bricks. The drivers were expected to average 16.2 miles per hour on long journeys, but with only 95 bhp available they had to belt them along and coast on suitable stretches of road, resulting in several spectacular pile ups.

Transport operations in those years were far removed from those of today. Then, the railways still moved vast quantities of goods on a much larger rail network. If a lorry driver was employed on 'long distance' then it usually meant he undertook journeys from say London to Manchester, or Leeds to Glasgow.

Such a trip would take him a day to complete as his lorry went along at the legal speed of 20mph. In fact most lorries at that time were capable of 28-30mph flat out, but low power-to-weight ratios would result in a fully laden lorry having to climb even a modest hill in second gear at approximately 7-8mph. A stiff climb over the Pennine routes or Shap Fell would often require crawler gear at 3mph. Tyre punctures and blow outs were frequent, and drivers were expected to change punctured wheels themselves, as well as carrying out any other running repairs as required.

Maximum gross weight vehicle weights were 12

tons for a four wheeler, 19 tons for a six wheeler, 22 tons for an eight wheeler or four wheeler drawbar lorry and trailer. Articulated outfits were rare and could gross up to 22 tons. Until 1942 eight wheelers had not been allowed to pull a drawbar trailer, but the war requirements caused the law to be changed. This increased the gross weight of the lorry and trailer by up to 10 tons.

The AEC Works Transport Department must have been the very first operator in the country to take advantage of this relaxation in the law, as at one minute past midnight on the appropriate day in 1942 one of their Mammoth Major Mk II 8 wheelers with drawbar trailer left Southall fully loaded with tank engines for Chilwell Ordnance Depot, near Nottingham. It was powered by an experimental 9.6 litre engine. In all instances of a trailer being pulled, then a second man or trailer mate had to be carried in the cab. One of his functions was to apply a brake lever which operated the trailer brakes mechanically, so assisting the main braking system of the lorry which was usually a servo-assisted hydraulic type of system. These maximum gross vehicle weights were to remain unchanged until 1955.

Above: James Gilmore of Liverpool shortened this Matador Mk II into a ballast tractor, seen here towing a crane. The protruding radiator suggests that it is fitted with a Gardner engine. The ornate lamp standard contrasts strangely with the row of derelict houses in the background. This AEC was originally in the fleet of J. Lyons & Co. Ltd. (*Arthur Ingram*)

Right: One of the 0344 Monarchs, fitted with the A186 engine, operated by Turners of Soham. This is a Park Royal cab, and note the different sized headlamps, typical of the period when only one was used in the dipped mode. Behind is a Mammoth Major Eight Mk II, one of several operated by the same firm. (*Arthur Ingram*)

Right: Harrisons of Dewsbury ran a nightly trunk between London and Yorkshire, and their Matador and Drawbar trailer heads out of the capital. The body is typical of the sort favoured by several Yorkshire hauliers; loading and unloading being possible through the roof of the van. (*Arthur Ingram*)

Right: Most AEC tractor units of this period were shortened rigids, and Hitchmans Dairies, from their premises on Walthamstow Avenue, North Circular Road London, operated this Duramin cabbed Monarch Mk II with a short tandem axle semi-trailer.
(*Arthur Ingram*)

Below: The well known large tanker operator, Bulwark Transport of Chippenham ran several makes of lorry including AEC. Bodied with a four compartment tank, their Mammoth Major Six Mk II travels through London.
(*Arthur Ingram*)

Right: Another member of the Davis Brothers' empire was Tozers transport, and this Mammoth Major Mk II was photographed outside their east London base. (*Arthur Ingram*)

Below: Some Mammoth Major Mk IIs received a deeper radiator at some time during their lifetime. A.E. Evans (Regent Transport) were almost an exclusive AEC fleet, with many of them being bought second hand from the major oil and petroleum distribution companies. (*Arthur Ingram*)

Right: The Gateshead firm of Orrell & Brewster were AEC operators from the 1930s until they faded from the scene in the 1980s. This photograph probably dates from the mid 1950s, shortly after the company had re-started after de-nationalisation. The Mammoth Major Eight Mk II is likely to be fitted with an A180 8.8 litre engine. (*Arthur Ingram*)

Below: Many building sites in the South East were visited by the Mammoth Majors of Marley Tiles, and in a typical London street scene of the period their well laden Mk II eight wheeler, with its hand loaded, straw packed, roofing tiles, heads the no.43 London Transport RT bus, up Holloway Road. (*Arthur Ingram*)

CHAPTER TWO

THE MARK III RANGE 1948~1953

By 1947 Southall was in full production with a full order book for both its passenger and goods vehicle ranges. The post war Labour Government had decreed that exports were to be the top priority for all manufacturing industry and AEC started to win large export orders with its new Mk III range of buses and lorries. Demand on the home market was outstripping the availability and customers had to wait a considerable length of time for the delivery of a new vehicle from the time it was ordered.

John Rackham, as Chief Engineer, was approaching the end of a brilliant and distinguished career at AEC. He had been appointed in 1928 from a similar post at Leyland Motors, although he had previously worked at AEC in its very early days. His career had then taken him on to working on tank design in the 1914-18 Great War, followed by some time in the United States of America. The Mk III goods vehicle range was to be his last direct contribution to AEC although his ideas and influence continued for many years after his retirement. His primary concern was the design of the chassis, engine and transmission, but he always liked to contribute his ideas to the designs of passenger vehicle bodies and lorry cabs. There was always a distinct family resemblance in the pre tilt-cab era between AEC lorries and buses, quite rare amongst such combined vehicle builders. Obviously, having such a distinctive badge as the famous blue triangle

prominently displayed on the radiator front grille helped. Although AEC goods vehicles were cabbed by a multitude of body builders, they were all supplied with design drawings by AEC and most copied them faithfully, with sometimes their own subtle variations.

Because Southall was at full chassis building capacity, the Mk III range offered basically the same types of vehicles as the Mk II range. John Rackham's approach to a new design was to start afresh, although there was obviously some overlap and continuation from earlier designs. The Monarch Mk III type 3451 was the maximum weight (12 tons) two axle rigid and was still powered by the A173 7.7 litre engine available in a choice of wheelbases depending on the application. The Matador Mk III type 3471, for drawbar work, received the A216 9.6 litre engine and a new 5 speed constant mesh gearbox. This vehicle became the Mandator Mk III type 3472 in 1950, and was offered for the first time as a purpose built tractor unit. The Mandator model name had been previously used in the 1930s for a specialist low height lorry, based on a passenger chassis. The Monarch Mk III continued until 1956 by when some 1,889 had been built and its demise also saw the end of the A173 7.7 litre engine as a main vehicle range power unit.

The flagship of the Mk III range was the Mammoth Major, particularly in 4 axle format, which with its exposed radiator became the classic representation of the British rigid eight. The Mk III was

listed as being available until 1960, but it was from the late 1940s until the mid-1950s that the majority of the total of 6,293 Mammoth Majors were built. The Mammoth Major Mk III differed in several important areas from the pre-war Mk IIs, and the post war Mammoth Major built between 1945-47 was really an interim model with some features common to both its predecessor and successor. The new Mammoth Major was powered by the A216 9.6 litre engine and the 5 speed constant mesh gearbox. The model type designation indicated the final drive option.

The six wheelers were type 3671 with single drive, double reduction spiral bevel axle: type 3671H with double drive bogie by overhead worm and wheel with third differential: and type 3671K with a fully articulated double drive bogie. Similarly the eight wheelers were type 3871 with single drive, double helical/double reduction spiral bevel axle: type 3871H with double drive bogie via overhead worm and wheel with third differential, and there was a choice of either a 4 spring or fully articulated rear bogie. The braking system was either a Clayton Dewandre or Westinghouse full air pressure system, with compressed air being provided by a novel single cylinder compressor attached to the rear of the gearbox and driven directly from the gearbox layshaft.

As was common on all eight wheelers at that time the second steering axle wheels were unbraked, and the multi-pull handbrake operated on the rear wheels. Brake drum diameters were reduced from 16¾" to 16½" to withstand the increased brake shoe pressures, whilst at the same time leaving the outer diameter suitable for the fitment of 20" diameter road wheels. This was the first British built goods vehicle chassis, from a high volume builder, to feature full air pressure brakes as standard (despite later claims to the contrary by Atkinson) and brought about a much needed improvement in braking performance.

Certainly with the eight wheeler and trailer combination becoming an increasingly popular option with operators since the 1942 relaxation of the law preventing such combinations, the traditional type of vacuum hydraulic braking systems were stretched to provide a consistent braking performance, particularly on long downhill descents or in emergency situations with an outfit which could legally gross up to 32 tons. AEC had fitted full air pressure brakes to a specialist tractor for use as an Australian road train prime mover in the early 1930s: also to several passenger vehicles before the war, and to the Matador 4 x 4 Artillery Tractor built from 1939-45.

As the multi-axle Mk IIIs entered service the AEC

Everard Transport Services Ltd. operated this Mammoth Major Eight which appears to be a Mk III. It is in fact a Mk II, type 0386, chassis number 917, which had been re-cabbed and had received a deeper radiator. It was new to Pickfords in August 1935, and went to Everards in August 1954. (*Arthur Ingram*)

North Eastern Scotland was the home of several noted haulage fleets, – Munro's Transport being one of them. They also had various depots, and their Mammoth Major Mk II, type 0386/20 from the immediate post-war years, is heading north out of London one evening on a trunk journey. *(Arthur Ingram)*

Area Service Engineers undertook a training programme for drivers to instil in them the fact that a soft pedal did not mean no brakes with an air pressure system. If the driver had a soft brake pedal with the vacuum hydraulic system, then he had a big problem!

One of the problems with the braking systems used on the Mk II vehicles, and particularly the 0836/20 models, was that the repeat usage of the footbrake, say on a long descent with a loaded vehicle, could result in the rear brake drums expanding to such an extent that the hydraulic rams would 'ratchet up', with the result that when the drums cooled down the brake shoes were hard on. There was no such ratchet with the Mk III system as the air chambers were chassis mounted. A full air pressure system, although carrying a small weight penalty was much more effective and efficient and simpler to maintain. Drivers of Mk IIIs could find themselves with insufficient air pressure on long descents if the brakes were out of adjustment, or if they had been using the foot brake too frequently at slow speeds. In consequence the familiar Westinghouse semaphore signal was fitted in the cab which told the driver to stop if it was activated by low air pressure. The Mammoth Major III undoubtedly set new braking standards and it was to be several years before AECs competitors began to match their braking performance.

An exhaust brake was also available as an optional extra.

The Author recalls that a driver called Gordon Axon once told him that he had witnessed a serious collision on the A5 near Hinckley in the late 1950s, and the road was blocked. He was running ahead to stop oncoming traffic round a bend and a Mammoth Major Mk III tanker belonging to A.E. Evans (Regent Transport) was approaching at full speed. Gordon had thought that it had no chance of stopping in time and that it would plough into the wreckage, but the tanker, which was fully laden, stopped well short of the accident and he felt sure that at the time no other make of lorry would have been able to stop in time.

The Mk III also had stronger springs giving it a characteristic slight nose down profile: this was an additional bonus to some operators. Peter Slater was a well known Yorkshire based coal haulier and his Mammoth Major Mk IIs were frequently stopped by the police for overloading, as they sat down at the rear end. The equally well-laden Mk IIIs escaped because they did not appear to be overloaded!

With the Mk IIIs the '2 sticker' transmission had gone, but this was lamented by some operators. Whilst in theory eight gear ratios were available with the system, AEC arranged it so that only five ratios were to

be used; 1-4 in low range, and 4 in high, but many operators got around this by modifying levers so that all the main gears could be used in either low or high range, (as with a modern Range change gearbox), so giving better vehicle performance. Some even turned the auxiliary gearbox around so giving a higher geared top range: rumour has it that some Mk IIs so geared were capable of 60 mph! With the straight 5 speed gearbox in the Mk III Mammoth Major, 38 mph was top wack, unless 'silent 6th' or 'Aberdeen Overdrive' was used, both terms referring to the practice of coasting out of gear on suitable stretches of road, even though the speed limit for a heavy lorry was still 20 mph at this time.

The Mk III chassis was heavier than its predecessor due to a thicker chassis frame section, heavier axles and springs, heavier engine and gearbox, as well as heavier road wheels with larger tyres. Depending upon the cab and bodywork fitted, the eight wheeler could legally carry around 14½ tons of payload within the 22 gross vehicle weight limit. If a trailer was being pulled then a further 7-8 tons of payload was the norm. As well as a flat platform load carrier and tipper chassis, the Mammoth Major Mk III eight wheeler also became a very popular tanker chassis with many bulk liquids carriers.

These were very significant years, not only for the development and growth of AEC, but for road transport operations as well. In 1948 AEC merged with both Maudslay and Crossley. Both were long established vehicle builders. Maudslay were based at Parkside

Works, Coventry, but they also operated a plant at Great Alne near Alcester, which had been a wartime 'shadow' factory. They built a high quality range of heavy goods vehicles and some passenger vehicles. Since the end of the war they had fitted AEC engines into most chassis, although some Mogul four wheelers received the Gardner 5LW engine. Their own 6 cylinder petrol engine had been fitted into sixty Marathon passenger chassis which were bodied as horse boxes and operated with the LNER at York. These gave the horses a very smooth and quiet ride.

Within four years of the merger with AEC, Maudslay's own vehicle range, including the Mogul and Meritor, had been phased out in favour of the Monarch and Mammoth Major respectively, although some 'badge engineering' was not uncommon, with purely AEC vehicles sometimes being badged as Maudslays. This merger in particular was beneficial to AEC, not only for the engineering capacity and expertise so gained, but it also provided some much needed additional chassis building facilities, and non-standard AECs were built by Maudslay at Parkside. Some of these non-standard types amounted to quite large build numbers including 350 Mammoth Major Mk III 6 wheelers for an Air Ministry contract. These refuelling bowsers had a non-standard wheelbase.

Crossley Bros. of Manchester and Stockport on the other hand, had ceased building goods vehicles by 1948, their last lorries being built during the 1939-45 war for the armed forces. In 1948 they were passenger vehicle builders using their own design of engine.

The BRS depot at Tufnell Park, London, is the setting for this early post-war Matador Mk III, type 0347, with its drawbar trailer. (*Arthur Ingram*)

The large Bradford based baking company, Newboulds, placed this Matador Mk III articulated tractor unit and step-frame semi-trailer in service in 1948. It was used for trunking duties to subsidary depots at Hull and Sheffield, and was similar to their Matador Mk II artics used in the months before D-Day in June 1944 (*see Chapter 5*). The design of the van was such that trays of bread were loaded onto carriers inside the body, loading being done manually through the rear door and side shutters. (*Motorphoto*)

Crossleys had their origins as a stationary and gas engine builder at the turn of the century. Park Royal Vehicles of north London, along with its subsidiary company Chas. H. Roe of Leeds was acquired in 1949. Both were bodybuilders, with Park Royal also building lorry cabs. During the 1930s AEC had taken over Monarco Engines, who made engine bearings, and The British Gear Grinding Company whose name adequately described their activities.

The two 1948 mergers were very complicated and led to AEC being renamed as Associated Commercial Vehicles Ltd., with the registered office being at 49, Berkeley Square, London. This was a holding company for the constituents of the group. The initials AEC were retained, with AEC Ltd. formed to assume the design, production and sales and marketing responsibilities of the old company. To all intents and purposes, to anyone connected with industry AEC was still AEC whatever its make-up was.

1948 was a significant year for road transport operators in Great Britain. On 1st January all transport firms involved in long distance operations were nationalised under the British Transport Commission, with separate Executives formed to run London Transport, British Railways, Docks and Waterways, and Road Transport. The Road Transport Executive was initially responsible for provincial buses, but these were

removed from its scope from June 1949, it then being renamed the Road Haulage Executive (RHE), trading as British Road Services, (BRS). The RHE had powers to acquire any transport company whose work was mainly long distance haulage. The formation of BRS was to have a significant influence on road haulage in Great Britain for the next 35 years, even though de-nationalisation occurred in 1953.

As the RHE got to grips with its gigantic task of organising the thousands of road haulage companies which were reluctantly nationalised, one of its longer term aims was to standardise on vehicle types for different aspects of its operations. AEC vehicles obviously performed well in comparison with other makes, because in the following years AEC were to supply thousands of lorries to BRS.

The introduction of the Mk III range heralded the start of a period during which AEC rapidly grew and became established as a leading builder, not only at home but overseas as well. It was the start of a period which can be described as a Golden Age, not only for AEC and its achievements during the years ahead, but also for road transport operations in Great Britain as the movement of freight by the railways rapidly began to decline, and the sight of the rigid eight wheeler, often with a trailer, became an increasingly common sight on the roads of the country.

Top right: To anyone who was familiar with the Liverpool transport scene in the immediate post-war years, this photograph will be pure nostalgia. Frank Seafield's new Monarch Mk III loads sacks of flour, with the driver, (probably Frank Seafield himself) 'hand balling' his load on. The smoke blackened warehouse walls, the cobblestone roadway, and the Sentinel steamer were all part of a richly varied Merseyside road haulage landscape then. (*Motorphoto*)

Right: Waste contractors, A. Pannell, had a large AEC fleet engaged in transferring London's rubbish to outlying tips and landfill sites. In the days before hydraulic refuse compactors, high capacity bodies were necessary for a decent payload to be obtained. (*Arthur Ingram*)

Middle left: Built at the Parkside, Coventry works of Maudslay, this 1952 Commercial Motor Show Majestic twin steer was obviously destined for an overseas customer. It shows how all AECs, at that time, left the assembly line, with cabs being fitted by various coach-builders at a later date. Twin steer six wheeler chassis had very little overhang behind the rear axle, in the interests of obtaining correct front axle loadings. (*Harry Pick collection*)

Bottom right: The Mammoth Major Eight Mk III was a very popular tanker chassis with all kinds of bulk liquid carriers. Whitbread the brewers had several for bulk deliveries to their bottling stores and depots. The eight wheeler tanker and drawbar trailer was not a common sight, except for those operated by the breweries. (*Arthur Ingram*)

Right: Smith & Robinson were based at Rothwell, near Leeds, and they were a large tanker company with a high proportion of AECs. This Mammoth Major Six Mk III was one of several, and like all tankers of that era it has the mandatory galvanised bucket swinging somewhere on the vehicle. (*Arthur Ingram*)

Below: Coupled to a short drawbar trailer, the Tate & Lyle Mammoth Major Eight Mk III still makes an impressive sight. The cab is by Express Motor Bodies. After several years of service with the parent company's fleet, many of these AECs then transferred to Silver Roadways, their transport subsidiary. (*Arthur Ingram*)

Left: For many transport enthusiasts of the 1950s period, the well sheeted and roped load on a rigid eight lorry is a delight to see. The BRS Mammoth Major Eight Mk III at Tufnell Park depot epitomises those long gone days beautifully. The AEC is also clean and tidy, all indications of a good, conscientious driver. (*Arthur Ingram*)

Bottom left: One of only a few Monarch Mk IIIs in the all-AEC fleet of Harold Wood & Sons Ltd. With their head office at Heckmondwike in West Yorkshire their vehicles operated out of several depots and could be seen anywhere in the country, as they carried bulk liquids for many of the major chemical and oil companies. The tanks on the Monarchs were not baffled, giving the driver an interesting ride if not quite full. (*Arthur Ingram*)

Right: The well known company of Samuel Williams appear to be using an old AEC rear axle as the dolly for transporting this long beam. With the load bearing point directly above the rear axle of the Monarch Mk III, then the front end of the lorry must have been light. (*Arthur Ingram*)

Right: Three large storage tanks transported by the lorries from the BRS Hampstead depot make an impressive convoy at rest outside the British Oxygen factory on the North Circular Road. The windscreens of this Mammoth Major Mk III are slightly larger, in an attempt to improve the vision for the driver. (*Arthur Ingram*)

Left: With a bulky, uneven load of bales or sacks securely sheeted and roped, a van probably full of parcels or small consignments has been hung on the back of Harrison's Mammoth Major Eight Mk III, as it heads out of London one evening. (*Arthur Ingram*)

Right: The board on the side of the tanker says that the load is Sodium Hydrochloride, and the tank is a typical acid or caustic carrying, rubber lined, design of the period. Murgatroyds were from Widnes, and the rounded style of cab on their Mammoth Major Eight Mk III was built by Bowyer Bros. of Congleton. (*Arthur Ingram*)

Allocated to the Milnsbridge, Huddersfield BRS depot, (pre-nationalisation Joseph Hanson Ltd.,) was this 1949 Mammoth Major Eight Mk III. It was photographed outside the premises of P. Conacher & Co. Ltd. laden with a church organ made by them and destined for Cape Town. (*J. Morris Bray*)

Below: After de-nationalisation, the Hanson transport business re-started, and these three Mammoth Major Eight Mk III tankers were placed in service on contract to the ICI Dyestuffs Division, also based at Huddersfield. (*J. Morris Bray*)

CHAPTER THREE

THE GOLDEN YEARS, PART ONE 1954~1958

By 1953 the Mk III range was selling in all markets and the companies merged with AEC a few years earlier had become well integrated into the Southall way of doing things. Home market demand was still quite good despite uncertainties about the proposed de-nationalisation of BRS. The supply situation with raw materials was now somewhat easier. The export side of the business was well established, although some bad debt problems had been experienced in some overseas markets. A larger capacity version of the by-then very reliable and very popular 9.6 litre engine had been produced in1949 to meet some export market requirements. It had an increased bore dimension of 130mm giving a swept volume of 11.3 litres, with larger inlet valves. It was rated at 150 bhp at 1,800 rpm and this engine began to attract the attention of many Mammoth Major eight wheeler operators, particularly where draw-bar trailers were being pulled.

The Mammoth Major with the A221 11.3 litre engine was only matched in the horse power stakes by Leyland, whose Octopus was powered by their slightly smaller 11.1 litre 0.680 engine, which was rated at 154 bhp at 2000 rpm. Both of these eight wheelers were more powerful than those built by competitors such as Atkinson, ERF, and Foden who fitted the much smaller 8.4 litre Gardner 6LW engine which was rated at 112 bhp at 1,700 rpm. The 'rigid eight' was undoubtedly King of the Road, although the first signs

of growth in demand for articulated vehicles was now being seen.

In 1951 a Conservative Government had been elected and one of its promises had been the de-nationalisation of many of the industries nationalised by the previous Labour administration. In May 1953 the Bill authorising the de-nationalisation of road transport received Royal Assent, but it had been conceded that the RHE could retain a lorry fleet of up to 13,900 tons (unladen weight) under State ownership. So the stage was set for a nationalised transport fleet (BRS) to compete with a private free enterprise fleet. Even so, the dice was still heavily loaded in BRS' favour to a large extent, as a 25 mile radius of operations limit for rival hauliers was not lifted until 1955.

The partial dismantling of BRS took most of 1953 and it was not until 1954 that private haulage fleets were able to re-start.

Disposal of BRS vehicles was done on a tender basis, either for complete (smaller) depots, or blocks of vehicles, which came with a special 'A' licence each, but no business goodwill, so even wrecked vehicles were tendered for, just to obtain the 'A' licence. Many former operators who had been forced to sell out in 1948 bought vehicles and re-commenced in business. The 'A' licence enabled them to carry any type of goods anywhere (after 1955) for hire or reward and were very much sought after. 'B' licences usually applied to hauliers involved in coal, roadstone, sand and gravel, and

The well known heavy haulage specialists, Sunter Bros. of Northallerton started to buy AECs after acquiring two AEC coaches for their passenger transport offshoot. This Tillotson cabbed Mammoth Major Six Mk III tractor unit is seen loaded with steel. The rear mudguards appear to have been fabricated from corrugated iron sheets. (*Arthur Ingram*)

milk collections etc., and restricted the operator to a certain radius (usually 25 miles, but in rural areas it could be 40 miles) of his operating depot. 'C' licences enabled a manufacturer to carry his own goods only, and the vehicles so licenced could not be used for hire or reward purposes. The 'A Contract' licence was a useful means by which an 'A' licence operator could increase his vehicle fleet without obtaining another 'A' licence, by dedicating a vehicle to carry for a specific customer only.

These details are mentioned in the context of this chapter because these events in 1953 and their consequences were to have a direct effect on AEC and the sales of its goods vehicles, as the privately owned road haulage sector started to expand rapidly, with any lorry the operator could obtain, whether it be new or second hand.

The AEC sales team realised that they had a large gap in their lorry portfolio. They had a highly respected and popular heavy vehicle range which was successful, with every vehicle capable of being produced at Southall and Maudslay being sold. The problem was that they had nothing to offer in the lighter vehicle market, which was becoming increasingly important in terms of numbers sold annually. Co-incidentally this dilemma also applied to the passenger range. Even if such an AEC lorry had been available, production capacity at Southall was not available to produce it. Fortunately the Maudslay plant at Great Alne was able to solve this particular problem. Leyland had shown the way with the successful Comet 75 introduced in 1947 and then the more powerful Comet 90 introduced in 1951.

Competing in the same 12 tons gross vehicle weight market as the AEC Monarch, the Comet 90 was some 1½ tons lighter and some 15 mph faster, giving it a tremendous productivity advantage over the Monarch. AEC gathered together all of its senior sales and engineering personnel, not only from Southall but from the regional depots also, at a London hotel for a three day conference to decide what they had to do to enable them to enter the lighter vehicle market. Many suggestions were put forward, including using a Bedford type of chassis. A prototype vehicle, based on a Commer chassis with a side valve petrol engine had actually been built, but fortunately reason prevailed and this very dated design never entered production. Out of this conference the specification of a new medium weight chassis called the 'Mercury' evolved, and it was to be powered by a new wet liner monobloc engine.

In 1935 AEC had produced a monobloc wet liner engine of 6.6 litres capacity designated type A172. This was a 6 cylinder engine and not to be confused with the 4 cylinder engine of similar capacity. Regrettably the A172 engine had earned itself the name of 'bootlace' because of its tendency to fail when driven hard. It was unusual in that it was designed to run either as a petrol or indirect diesel unit, and was aimed at certain operators who wanted a dual purpose vehicle: to run with a coach body and petrol engine for smoothness and quietness in summer: and to run with a lorry body and diesel engine in winter.

To change from one fuel to another required a change of cylinder heads. This engine had never been

Charringtons distributed for Mobil, and the 'tin-front' Mammoth Major Eight Mk III was the workhorse of many oil and petroleum distribution companies. This is a Park Royal cabbed version. By this time it was usual for the tanker's own diesel tank to be fitted on the offside of the chassis, so that access to the discharge couplings and valves for the driver was from the nearside. (Arthur Ingram)

very successful then, because of problems associated with the wet liners, but it had been sorted out to make a successful tank diesel engine during the war. For the Mercury this engine was re-designed as a direct injection unit becoming the A410 of 105 x 130mm cylinder dimensions or alternatively, the A470 of 112 x 130 mm cylinder dimensions. Respective swept volumes were 6, 754 litres for the A410, rated at 98 bhp at 2,000 rpm and 7,685 litres for the A470, rated at 112 bhp at 2,000 rpm.

Both engines could be had in horizontal format (AH) for the new Reliance coach, introduced at the same time, as well as the vertical (AV) format. From an engineering point of view wet cylinder liners are more desirable, as the engine coolant is in direct contact with the cylinder, so giving uniform and even cooling, but the engine block is a lot less rigid than a dry liner design (unless the block is of massive proportions) and there is a risk of distortion when the cylinder heads are tightened down onto the block. A new 5 speed synchromesh gearbox was matched to the new engine, with final drive through a new spiral bevel rear axle. A choice of wheelbase lengths was available, including a tractor unit, for different applications. The model and engine designations were new for AEC also. The type designation was GM4:– G=Goods vehicle, M=Medium weight, 4=4 wheeler: and the engine designation:– AV=Vertical engine, 470=Approximate engine capacity in cubic inches.

The Mercury was still heavier than the Leyland Comet 90: for instance it had heavier axles with 10 stud

wheels, whereas the Comet had 8 stud wheels, but it was more powerful and this was to become a great advantage when gross vehicle weights were raised in 1955. The cab was a new design and was initially built by Hampshire Car Bodies (HCB). Brakes on the very first models were a vacuum-assisted hydraulic system, then air hydraulic brakes were used. Production commenced in a new building at the Maudslay plant at Great Alne.

The early Mercurys had their share of problems. The gearbox was prone to failure by the synchromesh cones seizing up, mainly because drivers still insisted on double clutching on gear changes as they had to do with constant mesh gearboxes, and the early rear axle diffs were very weak, with crown wheels becoming detached until additional fixing bolts were incorporated. By the time the Mk II version (2GM4) was announced in 1956 these problems had been rectified and the full air pressure brake system installed to give the Mercury the best brakes in its vehicle class. The maximum gross weight for a 2 axle rigid lorry had been increased to 14 tons in 1955, and the Mercury now really came into its own as sales took off for it to become a top seller.

The larger AV470 engine was far more popular than the AV410 engine and this engine gave the Mercury 25 bhp more than the Leyland Comet 90 which is a significant amount of power at 14 tons gross vehicle weight operations, and it also had superior brakes. The AEC wet liner engine in the Mercury did gain a reputation for frequent cylinder head gasket failures, but much of this was due to bad driving practices such as

thrashing them along, or letting them labour at low revs on hills. If driven properly and sensibly then very high mileages between overhauls were possible without any problems.

There had been many sceptics at AEC about the decision to go 'down market' as they saw it, but the Mercury was still a high quality vehicle in the best AEC traditions, and it found favour with many heavy vehicle operators who wanted to standardise the lighter vehicles in their fleets to one make. It also found favour with the 'A' licence hauliers who needed a new low unladen weight, maximum gross vehicle weight lorry. Whilst the 'A' licence was much coveted, there were also strings attached to it: it was weight stipulated and determined the unladen weight of the lorry which could be operated with it, so the Mercury was an ideal choice where unladen weight was a limiting factor. Many haulage businesses re-started at this time chose the Mercury, either new or second hand, and as they expanded their fleets in subsequent years, or were able to operate heavier and larger vehicles, it was to the various AEC models that they turned.

Payload on a long wheelbase Mercury with an alloy platform body was a comfortable 9 tons within the 14 tons gvw limit. Top speed was 44 mph. As a result of the success of the Mercury the long serving Monarch was discontinued in 1956, although the model name was retained for use on export versions of the Mercury. In line with the increase in 2 axle lorry gross vehicle weights in 1955, the new gross vehicle weight for a six

wheeler became 20 tons, and for an eight wheeler, articulated tractor and semi-trailer, or four wheeler rigid plus drawbar trailer, 24 tons. The maximum gross weight for a rigid multi-axle lorry drawbar trailer remained at 32 tons. In 1957 the long standing 20 mph heavy vehicle speed limit was raised.

The introduction of the Mercury had seen a new style of cab upon an AEC, with its slightly bulbous and rounded front profile, the radiator was hidden behind a grille panel. This style was extended to the heavyweight Mammoth Majors and Mandators, which started to appear with the famous exposed radiator hidden away behind a grille panel. Those lorries so cabbed became known as 'Tin Front' and modernised the appearance of the AEC range.

These were very successful times for the AEC sales force as they now had a complete range of quality goods vehicles to offer. For years many own account fleets such as London Brick Company, Express Dairies, and Bowaters had operated large quantities of AECs, but growing haulage companies such as the Yorkshire based tanker operator Harold Wood were ordering Mammoth Majors and Mercurys in significant numbers. Harold Wood was to operate some 818 mammoth Majors alone in Mk II, III, and V versions. Road haulage was growing at an unprecedented rate as the dust of de-nationalisation settled. It was still very difficult for small hauliers to obtain 'A' licences: they could apply to the Traffic Commissioners for additional ones, but they had to be able to prove that a need for

The Majestic twin steer six wheeler was conceived and built at the Maudslay Division of ACV. They were built in small numbers from 1951-57, and were usually fitted with the A216 9.6 litre engine. The larger A221 11.3 litre engine was optional. (*AEC*)

Returning to Liverpool from London with empty crates and an unladen drawbar trailer. The driver and mate of the Mammoth Major Eight Mk III cast suspicious glances at the photographer, whose bicycle can be seen in the foreground. (*Arthur Ingram*)

them existed, and BRS, British Railways, and the Transport Trades Unions all had the right to oppose such applications. The aforementioned 'A Contract' licence was the means by which Harold Wood and many others expanded their businesses.

The AEC after-sales and service departments also played a huge part in these successful years. From early days AEC had realised the value of a good after-sales service and had established its own Sales, Service and Parts depots at strategic centres such as Southall, Nottingham, Bradford, Glasgow, St. Helens, and West Bromwich, leaving a network of distributors and agents to cover the entire country, with parts departments such as that well known facility at Page Street, Westminster.

The AEC depots from where teams of Sales personnel operated, also provided a 24 hour, seven days service for breakdowns, as well as a full spare parts service, and either a night shift or men on standby for call outs, who were prepared and equipped to deal with all eventualities whether it be the replacing of an injector pipe or a complete engine overhaul. Attached to, and operating from these depots was a Service Engineer whose brief was to visit all known operators of AECs Maudslays and Crossleys in his area on a regular basis, and at the same time to advise the operators on any problems they might be having with the vehicles in service. The information gleaned from the operators by the Service Engineers was reported back to Southall, and it was received there with great interest and no doubt played a vital role in the development of future

designs. Even though AEC had a standard vehicle range they could and would tailor individual vehicles to a customer's specific requirements, something which some major vehicle manufacturers in the 1990s are only just realising is important.

The AEC breakdown and repair service gained an envied and unmatched reputation for promptness and efficiency, and this level of after-sales service and commitment to customers built a tremendous customer loyalty which they enjoyed for most of their existence.

In 1957 AEC announced an addition to the goods vehicle range with the Mammoth Major Mk III-derived Dumptruk six wheeler. Designated as type 3673M it was a half-cabbed 10 cu.yd capacity specialist off-road going site vehicle. For many years the Scottish Land Development Company Ltd., held the sole concessionary selling rights for the AEC Dumptruk range.

The lorry driver's job was still very much the same as it had been immediately after the war. There were no motorways, and long journeys took a long time. There were still plenty of old lorries on the roads but the new ones were more powerful, faster, and in the case of AECs, had powerful and efficient brakes. Cabs were still noisy and uncomfortable: some were now fitted with heaters, but the majority were still cold and draughty work places in winter, and too hot in summer. To be an AEC driver then was to be one of an elite band of men, as they were generally recognised to be one of the best makes of lorry on the road. Many would say they were the best.

Right: The smart looking Mandator Mk III of the prominent Monks International Transport fleet reverses its tanker semi-trailer into the cleaning bay at Whitbread brewery prior to loading with beer for Belgium. It has gained a bumper bar similar to those fitted to the contemporary Fodens. (*Arthur Ingram*)

Below: 'Susan Ann' was one of several AECs operated by Cussons of Kersal Vale, Salford, and impressive vehicles they were. This is a Park Royal cabbed Mammoth Major Eight Mk III, and it is interesting to note that the direction indicators are positioned on the front corners of the van body, and not on the cab. (*Arthur Ingram*)

Right:
Photographed
alongside the lorry
which brought
about its eventual
demise, the
Monarch Mk III was
heavier and slower
than the Leyland
Comet 90, and
these factors led to
the introduction of
the AEC Mercury in
1953. They were
parked at a cafe on
the A13 near
Thurrock.
(*Arthur Ingram*)

Below: Many of the
West Yorkshire
hauliers operated
specially bodied
lorries for the local
woollen trade. To
facilitate the loading
and unloading of
bales at the multi-
storey mills, these
van bodies had an
open roof, which was
sheeted over.
Mammoth Major
Mk III, number 174
in the Hanson fleet,
with a conventional
draw bar trailer,
climbs a cobbled
street in its home
town of Huddersfield.
(*J. Morris Bray*)

Top right: This Majestic is badged as a Maudslay and it is coupled to an Eagle drawbar trailer. It is equipped with vacuum-hydraulic brakes. In the days of steel rationing and Ministry of Supply allocations, if steel was allotted specifically to Maudslay, then the vehicles built from it would have to be badged accordingly. (*Arthur Ingram*)

Middle right: Not long in service when photographed delivering a load of fuel oil to a bus garage, this Mammoth Major Eight Mk III was based in the Grimsby area. The 'Jet' company logo is a reminder of the 1950s when delta winged aircraft were in fashion. (*AEC*)

Bottom right: The Lyons group of companies had memorable liveries for their vehicles. The two Mammoth Major Eight Mk IIIs are fitted with the Hampshire Car Bodies interim style of cab, which was an attempt to modernise the Mk III. The slogan for their ice cream is certainly not one for the health conscious 1990s! (*Arthur Ingram*)

Right: One of the memorable names of post war transport was J.W. Capstaff Ltd. of Newcastle, and they were eventually taken over to become a part of the short-lived Hilton Transport Services. The driver of this Mammoth Major Eight Mk III casts an anxious glance at Arthur Ingram as he heads north from London. A full load of fruit apparently has little effect on the strengthened rear springs of the Mk III chassis. (*Arthur Ingram*)

Below right: The contrast between the cab styles of the Mk III and the Mk V Mammoth Major is highlighted with this docklands photograph of two bulk grain carriers from the fleet of William Simmons Ltd. The lower chassis height of the Mk V (see chapter four) is also apparent, as it is carrying a much deeper body. (*Arthur Ingram*)

Above: The Mammoth Major Six Mk III of David Yule of Dyce loads 'brown reels' of paper; the width of which suggests that they could be imported, as they are resting on the side rails of the 7' 6" wide body. Most British paper mills produced such reels narrower, their average weight being some 1½ tons each. (*AEC*)

Left: Even new lorries in the mid 1950s were not required to have direction indicators fitted. The HCB cabbed Mandator Mk III is loaded with packing cases for Rome, Copenhagen, and New York, which would probably mean at least a full days waiting at three different docks to unload. (*AEC*)

Right: Fitted with the A221 11.3 litre engine, this was one of the Mandator Mk IIIs of John Wyatt Jnr. which ran regularly to Italy. This one was supplied to J.T. Hunt of Worksop, and is believed to have been the only AEC ever operated by them. Note the twin air horns and the Mercury bumper bar. (*Chris Wyatt*)

Below: Although this superb photograph appeared in 'Drawbar Outfits' by Peter Davis, (*Roundoak Publishing*), no apologies are made for reproducing it again. When photographed, this Mammoth Major Mk III eight wheeler and trailer was loaded with what was claimed to be the largest load of wool carried by Hansons. Also of interest is the fact that fleet number 159, when new, had operated as a tanker on contract to ICI Dyestuffs Division. (*J. Morris Bray*)

In production, the Mk III derived Dumptruk became a half-cab design, and the fuel tank was located behind the cab to reduce the chances of damage. Single rear wheels were fitted, but they still retained the high standards of AEC finish, with wheel nut rings and rear hub cover logos. (*AEC*)

Below: An early
Mercury Mk I with
HCB cab, which
was almost flush
fitting to the front
wings. Western
Transport of
Bristol operated
this one on a
regular job for the
former Bristol
Aircraft Company,
running between
their Filton and
Sunderland
factories. It is seen
here loading for a
local distribution
run with H.J.
Heinz products.
(*Veale & Co.
for AEC*)

Left: With a low loader semi-trailer and crane on board, this Mercury belonging to Dallas of New Malden was probably operating close to its 18 ton gross train weight limit. In less safety conscious days, the mate is content to lean on an open passenger door, and the crane driver sits on the trailer. (*Arthur Ingram*)

Top right: BRS started to buy Mercury tractor units in quantity shortly after its introduction in 1953. Photographed here is an early Mk I fitted with BRS specified 8 stud wheels with 8.25x20 tyres instead of the standard 10 stud wheels and 9.00x20 tyres. The braking system was a vacuum assisted hydraulic type, and many of these tractors had automatic couplings instead of fifth wheels. For many years, even into the late 1960s, BRS used vacuum braked trailers, which necessitated in later Mercurys being equipped with compressors and exhausters to enable them to couple up to any type of semi-trailer. (*Arthur Ingram*)

Right: The prototype Mammoth Major Mk III Dumptruk, type 3673M, equipped with a blade, is put through its paces at a colliery. (*AEC*)

Below: When this interesting photograph was taken the aeroplane and the old lorry on the Mercury represented a bygone age of transport. Now, the Mercury itself depicts another era, and it shows the slightly narrower profile of the later cabs. (*AEC*)

Left: New in April 1957, Ken Durston drove this 2GM4R Mercury for the next three years. The cab was made by Oldlands (Mk I), and the legal payload was 9½ tons, although more was frequently carried. Here it is loaded with aircraft parts bound for South Africa, via London Docks. Ken comments "it was like driving a Rolls Royce, with full air pressure brakes, although the air tank could freeze up in winter. She would walk away with the weight, and I also collected several speeding fines and endorsements". *(Ken Durston)*

Above: J. & A. Smith of Maddiston operated one of the largest privately owned fleets in Britain, with several depots in England and Scotland. So typical of the period is their Mercury and its 4-in-line semi-trailer. *(AEC/Motorphoto Archive)*

Left: The family firm of Thomas Harwood, Bolton, always turned out their AECs immaculately, with a cream and red livery, and gold leaf sign-writing. Just delivered from the body builder and paint shop, this 2GM4R Mercury (PBN 995) dates from early 1957, and at that time direction indicators were not compulsory. It also just pre-dates the increase in speed limits, as a 30 mph limit is written on the fuel tank. The author came to know this AEC very well in its later service with Raymond Holden, of Little Lever, who traded it in 1968 for a new tilt-cab Mercury. *(Thomas Harwood)*

Left: R. Hanson & Son Ltd. from Wakefield were coal and general haulage contractors. Their smart Mercury Mk II has had the body dropsides removed and is well laden with pre-fabricated steel sections. (*AEC*)

Below: Photographed in the early 1960s, this Percy Henley Mercury, fully loaded with hops, makes an evocative picture as it passes the oast house of the hop farm. (*Jack Henley*)

CHAPTER FOUR

THE GOLDEN YEARS, PART TWO 1959~1964

The late 1950s heralded a time of almost hectic expansion of AECs business both at home and overseas. The home market demand for goods vehicles was steadily increasing and this started to offset the decline for traditional double deck buses. Bus sales generally were in decline because of a decrease in passenger loadings due no doubt to the growing affluence of the population as car ownership became more common. In particular, the demand for tractor units was good as more and more operators introduced articulation into their fleets. As tractor units took up less space on the production line than a rigid, then goods vehicle output was able to increase.

Articulated goods vehicles had been used since the very earliest days of motorised transport and for many years Scammell had been the leading producer. Many articulated vehicle users were low loader operators, or companies involved in light weight local distribution work such as the railways. AEC tractor units were not uncommon, but until the 1950s they were usually conversions made by cutting down four wheelers such as Mammoths, Monarchs and 4 x 2 Matadors. Until 1955 there had been no real advantage in articulation at the heavier end of general road haulage operations. They also had a bad reputation for poor stability and a tendency to jack-knife, and it wasn't until braking systems were re-designed to allow better balance between the tractor

unit and semi-trailer braking systems that this fault was cured.

There was no difference in permissible maximum weights between a solo rigid eight wheeler and an articulated tractor and semi-trailer even after 1955, both being rated at 24 tons. The overall length of the latter was increased to 35 feet, which made a 26 ft. semi-trailer a possibility, although tractor unit wheelbases were typically 8-9 ft. Operators began to perceive that better vehicle utilisation was possible by using articulated vehicles, and initially it was in the medium weight Mercury sector that articulation rapidly increased. As a tractor unit the Mercury was initially rated at 18 tons gross vehicle weight, giving a payload of 12 tons. The Mandator was rated at 24 tons gross vehicle weight, and typically with a 24 or 26 ft. twin oscillating axle semi-trailer, (more commonly known as a '4-in-line' trailer) 15-16 tons of payload was possible. This was roughly the same payload as a Mammoth Major eight wheeler, but the Mandator was more flexible as it could be used, for instance, on night trunk duties and daytime journey work simply by swapping semi-trailers and drivers.

As the move to articulation rapidly grew, then the days of the rigid eight wheeler as a general haulage lorry were numbered, although it was always going to remain popular as a tipper and tanker chassis. The bulk haulage of products such as flour, cement, and sugar had now started, making the eight wheeler an ideal carrier of these heavy and dense commodities.

In 1959 AEC introduced a new heavy vehicle range, the Mk V. There was no Mk IV goods range because when the medium-weights had been introduced in 1953, it had been intended to call them the Mk IV range. However, as the medium-weight types incorporated both lorries and passenger vehicles, and as by then a heavy-weight Mk IV passenger range was already in production, this designation could not be used for the medium-weights as well, and a new type and numbering system was introduced (see Chap.3). When the passenger range progressed to Mk V, this designation was used for the new heavy goods range also, which was an entirely 'clean sheet' design.

To explain why this was so, it is necessary to return to 1934 and the very first AEC eight wheeler.

AEC were determined to win the race to have the first internal combustion engined eight wheeler on the road, so they used the existing Mammoth Major six wheeler chassis, the Mk I, type 668, and added a second steering front axle. This axle was of a somewhat lighter low beam type used on the contemporary Regent Mk I bus chassis, and it was attached with lighter road springs to accommodate the lower height of the Mammoth Major chassis to the point of attachment. In the interests of weight saving and other associated factors this second, or auxiliary axle, as it was then referred to, was not equipped with braking equipment, and this feature continued throughout the Mk II and Mk III series. During the war years several long wheelbase Matador Mk II lorries had been converted to twin steer six wheelers with a similar, but braked front axle assembly and steering gears. They operated satisfactorily at 16 tons gross vehicle weight, but a problem was encountered later when Construction and Use Regulations called for a mechanical hand brake operating on at least 50% of the vehicle's axles. The then standard AEC hydraulically operated, fixed cam, brake design did not readily lend itself to adaptation for a mechanical hand brake, and this was one factor which no doubt contributed to AECs' reluctance to produce a twin steer six wheeler for many years.

By the mid 1950s operators were suggesting that the Mk III range was becoming dated. Within the ACV Group, Maudslay had been producing a goods vehicle range with a decidedly more modern cab, with curved front panels, and a flush fitting radiator and headlamps. The main eight wheeler competitor, the Leyland Octopus, was fitted with a modern, flush fronted, all metal cab. Some AEC cab builders, and operators themselves, had produced adaptations of the standard cab in an attempt to update it .

AEC, in conjunction with one body builder introduced what was referred to as an interim cab with flush front panels, and they went on to equip Mk III chassis with a pressed steel, domed front panel assembly to enclose the existing style radiator with a fabricated grille similar to that used on the medium weight range and passenger vehicles. Known as the 'Tin Front' cab it

was prone to rattles, and in the opinion of many operators it did not achieve what they were looking for. Basically the cab itself had not changed, being of composite construction, and it was still cramped, noisy, and uncomfortable, whilst the problem of poor visibility for tall drivers, due to a low top windscreen rail continued. Several tanker operators including Smith and Robinson, and Harold Wood, both of whom operated large fleets of Mammoth Majors in Mk II and Mk III versions, felt that the centre of gravity was high with the existing spring arrangement, and there was a problem with excessive rear axle hop when brakes were applied when unladen.

The mighty Mammoth Major had long been the best seller in the AEC range of goods vehicles and at the 1958 Commercial Motor Show, AEC announced that it intended to maintain its lead in this field by displaying the Mk V heavy goods vehicle range. These new Vehicles incorporated many improvements over their predecessors, including new engines of either 590 or 690 cubic inches capacity, a new cab, retracted front axles giving better access to the driving cab, improved braking, and a new rear bogie as well as many detail improvements. In effect the generous 12" x 3" by $\frac{5}{16}$" chassis frame members of the old Mk III models were upturned, bringing the tapered flange at the front end on top to provide a level datum line for the attachment of suspension brackets. This also provided better access to the engine auxiliaries. The heavy crossmember of the Mk III was eliminated, as were the dumb irons and engine banjo crossmember brackets, being replaced with vibration resilient mountings for the engine and gearbox. Identical front axles were fitted under the eight wheeler, with larger identical front road springs with double acting telescopic shock absorbers fitted to ensure good stability under varying load and road conditions.

At the rear end the choice was either a compensating underslung 4 spring suspension, or alternatively a fully articulated 2 spring rear bogie.

The Mammoth Major Eight Mk V chassis which was immaculately finished for the 1958 Commercial Motor Show. AEC staff spent weeks in preparing these show chassis, and the number of chromium plated items shows that no expense had been spared as well. (AEC)

Any mention of large AEC fleets must include the London Brick Company who operated many hundreds in over 50 years of association with Southall. In the days before lorry mounted cranes and self-stack systems, the bricks were loaded and unloaded by hand, and typically LBC carried 7000 on a Mammoth Major Eight Mk V such as this. (*AEC/Motorphoto Archive*)

applications, with the six wheeler being available as a heavy haulage tractor unit with a 40 tons gross train weight rating. A choice of final drive and rear suspension layouts were also available and these were designated:–

S suffix: single axle drive via double reduction spiral bevel double helical gearing and compensated 4 spring suspension.

D suffix: two axle drive via overhead worm reductions units with lockable third differential, and compensated 4 spring suspension.

The new engines, designated AV590 or AV690 differed considerably from the 9.6 and 11.3 litre units they replaced, whilst retaining similar dimensions. They were stronger and lighter, and of monobloc construction with wet cylinder liners. Their main and big end bearings were pre-finished and there were many other detailed improvements. The well proportioned high tensile forged steel crankshafts were dynamically balanced to close limits for higher constant engine speeds and a torsional vibration damper was fitted at the front end. In original form the AV590 engine was rated at 125 bhp at 1,500 rpm, and the AV690 produced 150bhp, also at 1,500 rpm, but they were later uprated with the addition of balance weights on each crankshaft webb, and the fitting of distributor type fuel pumps. Now designated 2AV etc., the power ratings were 159 bhp for the 2AV590, and 192 bhp for the 2AV 690, both at 2,000 rpm. The respective torque output figures were 430 lb.ft. at 1,100 rpm and 505 lb.ft. at 1,200 rpm. These engines operated well within their capabilities since records show that a turbo-charged version of the 690 was available for industrial and some overseas road going applications, rated at 250 bhp at 2,000 rpm, with 674 lb.ft.of torque at 1,200 rpm.

These engines all had 'flat torque curve' characteristics to give a good engine performance across the engine revs. range. A large clutch of 262 sq.ins. total frictional area was fitted, and the gearbox was either a 5 speed or 6 speed overdrive constant mesh unit.

Other features included power assisted steering, at first optional and then standard, and optional braking on all four axles of the eight wheeler instead of just the leading axle and rear bogie. These new models were designated as type G6R (goods, six wheel, right hand control) or G6L (left hand control for overseas markets) and type G8R and L for the eight. They were available with a choice of wheelbase lengths for various

W suffix: two axle drive via overhead worm and wheel units, with a lockable third differential, and a fully articulated 2 spring bogie.

A selection of axle ratios to suit individual operators were also available.

The braking system was an improved and uprated version of the Mk III system, with compressed air being provided by an engine mounted twin cylinder Clayton Dewandre or Westinghouse compressor, with a direct acting control valve activating the 'S' cam and roller brakes. These brakes provided a generous total frictional area of 1,205 sq.ins. for the standard three axle braked models, and was considerably greater with the four axle braked eight wheeler option. Brake drum diameters were 15½" with 4¾" wide front, and 7¾" wide rear brake shoes.

However, instances of rapid brake lining wear and brake drum crazing were soon experienced by some operators, and it was not long before a considerable weight saving and improvement in braking efficiency, along with increased brake lining life was achieved by the fitting of Girling brake assemblies. This, together with improvements to the engine and other details caused the model range to be designated 2G series. An option was a split front/rear braking system to safeguard against total brake failure, and an exhaust brake was also an optional extra on most models. Depending on the type of body fitted up to 16½ tons of payload could be carried within the legal 24 tons gross vehicle weight limit.

Complementary to the multi-axle Mk V range was the Mandator Mk V. Designated type G4RA (later 2G4RA), and this was available as a short wheelbase tractor unit or medium or long wheel base load carrier for use as either a heavy duty tipper, or for haulage operations with a drawbar trailer. It was not particularly common in the home market as a solo load carrier by reason of the high unladen weight. The Mandator shared many of the Mammoth Major components for fleet interchangeability and maintenance considerations. Final drive was through a heavy duty, double reduction spiral bevel double helical geared rear axle, with a choice of ratios to suit operator requirements. The tractor unit was originally introduced with a 8'1" wheelbase, but this was soon increased to 10'1" to take better advantage of the Construction and Use Regulations for tractor and semi-trailer.

With a design gross weight of 36 tons the Mandator Mk V was well on top of its job for operations at 24 tons gross train weight, and as such became extremely popular, with most operators choosing the higher powered AV690 engine with no weight penalty.

Payload, depending upon the size and type of semi-trailer was similar to the Mammoth Major eight wheeler running solo.

The Mk V range carried a completely new design of cab made of one piece glass fibre reinforced plastic, manufactured by the ACV Goup company, Park Royal Vehicles. It was located onto a new, steel cab structure, which was resiliently mounted to withstand vibration onto the chassis. Alternatively, an all aluminium on timber composite cab was available, depending upon operator choice. The front panel of this new cab carried the by now familiar AEC fabricated grille assembly, and was of a most attractive appearance. It was a considerable improvement over its predecessor, but its somewhat tapered styling resulted in it being cramped inside and there was no sound deadening incorporated. However, access forward of the front wheels was excellent, as was visibility. The old, exposed, heavy and costly radiator had gone, mourned by many, and was replaced by a much lighter and cheaper film block type. Coolant replenishment was through a non-detachable external filler cap.

Park Royal Vehicles were unable to meet the demand for cabs, and many were built by Tillotsons and Road Transport Services. Large operators such as Harold Wood built many of their own cabs.

When introduced the Mk V was an up to the minute, modern, heavy vehicle range, and was very successful and popular. Until Mk V production got into full swing, the heavier Mk IIIs continued to sell for another 18 months or so, until production of these famous models ceased in 1960.

By the mid 1950s sales of the various Mercury models, with by then most of the original problems eradicated, rocketed and the 2GM model was well established as a market leader. Even so there was a desire for increased payloads, and many operators felt that the AV470 engine was capable of coping with higher gross weights. In order to achieve this they turned to companies who were offering third axle conversions. One such company was Boys of Walsall

who had been offering such conversions on many makes of chassis for many years, but the conversion used on many Mercurys could only be regarded as crude.

With a poorly extended frame and an in-house produced, unequal length balance suspension, the trailing third axle was equipped with non-standard hubs, and cable operated wedge brakes. This resulted in un-balanced braking with considerably reduced overall efficiency when the vehicle was laden. Other problems were severe axle hop, and a lack of adhesion, sometimes with serious consequences when unladen.

Similar third axle conversions were offered by Primrose, Unipower, and York who all converted medium and long wheelbase Mercurys for 6 x 2 operations. All of this led to demands from operators for AEC to produce their own medium weight six wheeler vehicles but production capacity was at a premium. As a result of a customer request, the ingenuity and resourcefulness of the management and workshop staff at the AEC depot at Nottingham produced a decent 6 x 2 Mercury using standard and identical hubs and brake equipment on both rear axles. In this instance use was made of the then newly imported American Hendrickson rubber suspension bogie components attached to the extended and flitched Mercury chassis frame. A trailing axle was made up using standard AEC stub ends to enable Mercury rear hubs to be used. Wedge type Girling brake assemblies, as used on certain early Mercury Mk I vehicles were utilised, with the hand brake being connected by flexible cables. When completed this Mercury six wheeler went to work, and when Southall heard about it they decided that it could form the basis for a medium weight six wheeler. Subsequently, from 1960, similar models were produced by AEC, but with double drive Eaton Hendrickson units, and this model was called the Marshal, type GM6RHB, or GM6LHB in its left hand control guise. They retained the braking system of the prototype, with full air pressure operated front axle brakes, and air assisted hydraulic brakes on the rear axles.

The Eaton Hendrickson bogie gave a very harsh

The driver of the Beresford Mandator Mk V reverses under the 4-in-line semi-trailer loaded with ceramic tiles. This company was not a big AEC operator, preferring the products of Cheshire and Lancashire based manufacturers. (AEC/Motorphoto Archive)

With twin fuel tanks and a well sheeted load of paper, the Nichols Mammoth Major Six Mk V looks every inch a long distance lorry of the period. The driver was one of the few at that time to have a radio fitted in his cab, but he would require plenty of blankets on the engine cover to make it audible. (AEC)

ride, and in tipper format severely stressed the chassis frame and crossmembers, often resulting in cracking. To save weight a 6 x 2 Marshal (the Marshal name was revived from a very successful 6 x 4 chassis built for the War Department in the 1930s) was produced incorporating a York independent trailing axle, but this again did not prove to be entirely satisfactory. Many operators happy with the front end of the 2GM Mercury chassis and not wanting to, or able to, move up to the heavy vehicle range Mammoth Major V 2G6R, suggested that a medium weight 6 x 2 or 6 x 4 could be produced with the old and discarded compensated 4 spring arrangement of the by then obsolete Mk III range. Southall engineers decided that this would have been a retrograde step, and went on to produce 6 x 2 and 6 x 4 Marshals using the standard Mk V compensated 4 spring underslung suspension. Using this suspension, type 2GM6RAS was the single drive version, (double reduction, spiral bevel double helical axle), and type 2GM6RAT was the double drive version, (single reduction spiral bevel axles). Both proved to be very popular and successful in service.

The type 4GM6RS with full air pressure brakes on all axles introduced in 1964, was designed to operate at 22 tons gross vehicle weight to take advantage of an impending increase in weight limits. This was a 2 tons increase over the previous Marshal rating, which in its longest wheelbase form, with an aluminium alloy platform body already gave a payload of 14 tons when operated at 20 tons gross vehicle weight.

During the late 1950s and early 1960s, in response to the growing popularity of tractor units and articulated semi-trailers, and the increased payloads they offered, the AEC depots, along with some AEC distributors, converted many medium and long wheelbase 2GM Mercurys to 8' 9" wheelbase tractor unit rated at 18 tons gross train weight. This particular conversion was not altogether easy as the chassis frame side members were swept in forward of the rear axle to accommodate 10.00 x 20 wheel and tyre equipment, within an overall width of 7' 6". This sweep, together with crossmembers had to be transferred forward to the

rear of the cab. Later versions of the Mercury tractor unit with the new 5 or 6 speed constant mesh gearbox to replace the existing 5 speed synchromesh unit, were rated at either 18 or 22 tons gross train weight, depending upon the type of final drive, either a single or double reduction spiral bevel axle. The 22 tons version could give up to a very useful 15 tons of payload. Also available as an option in the 4GM4RA tractor unit with the 5 speed gearbox, was an Eaton 2 speed rear axle. This option was not altogether successful as constant cracking of the fabricated axle casing was experienced by many operators. The new D197 6 speed overdrive constant mesh gearbox and single speed rear axle produced a similar overall gearing, and this gearbox was offered across the range in 1962.

To cope with increased operating weights, the power ratings of the AV470 engine were first increased to 126 bhp at 2,000 rpm, and later to 138 bhp at 2,200 rpm. At these higher power outputs cylinder head gasket failures became prevalent, and in an endeavour to overcome this problem, which was becoming quite serious, modified holding down studs and nuts capable of increased torque loadings were fitted, together with a variety of different types of cylinder head gaskets. A full air suspension (from the contemporary Reliance coach) was used on some Mercurys, and 40 such vehicles entered service with the London Brick Company, fitted with an attractive Mk V style of cab, built by Road Transport Services.

In 1956 a twin steer version of the 2GM Mercury had been introduced for operations at 18 tons gross vehicle weight. This model had been developed by the ACV Group's Maudslay engineers who had previous experience of producing a successful vehicle of this configuration, called the Mustang. This name was carried over to chassis type GM6RH. It featured an air operated hydraulic system with wedge type Girling brake assemblies. This arrangement was more suited to hand brake operation on the second front axle brakes, for which it will be recalled the standard AEC brakes were not suitable. Production of this model continued until 1961 when some 350 chassis had been produced, many of them for tanker operations.

Such was the popularity and success of the Mercury and its derivatives, that by 1964 almost 10,000 had been built and over 1000 Marshals had also entered service.

In 1961 ACV had announced the takeover of Thornycroft who were based at Basingstoke. This takeover provided AEC with some much needed extra capacity, and the Thornycroft range of goods vehicles was quickly phased out in favour of the AEC range. Thornycroft continued to produce and develop their specialist Nubian vehicles and the gigantic Mighty Antar tank transporter for the army. Their gearbox production capacity became especially useful to AEC.

In August 1961 a £½ million extension was opened at Southall which was to be the finished chassis

inspection and despatch department. A new depot was also opened in Glasgow. A new 'super finishing' process for crankshaft production was installed at Southall, and the total production area then exceeded 1 million square feet.

On 5th June 1962 the commercial vehicle industry was stunned by the announcement that ACV and Leyland had agreed to merge. Both companies had large export markets and were often competing for the same orders, so the rationale for the merger was an attempted consolidation of the export activities, rather than head to head competition. AEC themselves were no strangers to takeovers and mergers, and in the 1950s there had been talks with BMC which had come to nothing. Had such a merger occurred then, it would probably have been beneficial to both companies, with the lighter BMC commercial vehicle range complementing the AEC heavy range.

When the ACV and Leyland merger was announced, the ACV Group shares price had been falling on the stock market. Whilst the AEC goods vehicles had been selling well, investors had been concerned about the falling bus orders. Also, in a short period of time AEC had invested large amounts of capital in several overseas ventures which were only slowly coming to fruition. Because of this, the company was short of investment capital and was vulnerable to a takeover approach, although it was in no way financially unstable. Leyland had always held shares in many rival companies and they shrewdly increased their shareholding in the ACV Group at this time. Leyland were producing more vehicles than AEC in total, but the overall AEC business was wider in scope, and the new Leyland Motor Corporation as it was named, had total assets in 1962 of £135 million, a massive group at that time.

For a while, at least outwardly, AEC carried on in much the same way as before, but Leyland gradually became the dominant partner and the engineering headquarters was established at Leyland to handle all major new developments for the group. Bob Fryars, who had become Chief Engineer at AEC was appointed Chief Engineer for the group's truck division. Donald Stokes

(later Lord Stokes) had been a successful Sales Director at Leyland, and he eventually became Chairman of AEC and the whole group.

Throughout these years the range of AEC's business had been steadily growing with engines being supplied for many purposes, including those sold to other vehicle builders. The horizontal version of the AEC 11.3 diesel engine was supplied in quantity to British Railways for powering Diesel Multiple Units. The specialist Dumptruck range was expanded after the initial success of the Mk III derived Dumptruk. Two more versions were introduced, the smaller one being the 690 Dumptruk, type DBK6RAB, which was based on the Mammoth Major Mk V six wheeler, although with a heavily strengthened chassis. It was a normal control, bonneted vehicle powered by the 2AV690 engine at standard power rating. Drive was through a D205 5 speed constant mesh gearbox, and a double reduction spiral bevel double helical, double drive bogie. With a design gross weight of 24.5 tons its Edbro tipping gear could reach its 70° body tipping angle in 13 seconds with a 10 cu.yd., 13½ tons payload. It proved to be a successful and popular design.

Big brother to this was the massive 18 cu.yd., capacity AVT 1100 powered Dumptruk, type DK4RA, designed and developed by Maudslay at Great Alne. It was a 2 axle 41 tons gross weight design. Power was from a turbo-charged 4 valve per cylinder 17.9 litre AEC engine, rated at 300 bhp at 1,900 rpm, and producing 966 lb.ft. of torque at 1,300 rpm. It was an oversquare design of engine of 155.6 x 155.6mm cylinder dimensions, and was also available in turbo-charged format as an industrial engine. Power was taken through an 18 inch clutch and 10 speed close ratio Fuller range change constant mesh gearbox to a heavy duty double reduction rear axle. The wheelbase

The Mammoth Major Eight Mk V continued to be as popular a tanker chassis as its predecessor had been, and with a lower chassis height the stability was better. Guinness operated a smart fleet of Mk Vs. (Arthur Ingram)

Arriving at its destination in Italy is this 1962 Mammoth Major Eight Mk V and drawbar trailer of John Wyatt. After the long journey from England it still looks smart, apart from some road dust. The refrigerated containers are of the demountable type. (*Chris Wyatt*)

was 11' 6", unladen height was 12' (10' laden), and the tipped height of the body was 21' 2". The unladen weight was 20 tons and the 18 cu.yd., 21 tons of payload, could be tipped by a body angle of 70° in 12 seconds by the Edbro tipping gear.

The front axle was rated at 13½ tons, and the rear axle at 27½ tons. Based on the American Euclid design, these monsters were not entirely successful, and many of the engines ended their days powering generators. The A1100 engine was also used in Railcars, sometimes in turbo-charged format. The Scottish Land Development Company Ltd., handled all the home sales for the Dumptruk range.

A large purchaser of AEC engines was the British Crane and Excavator Corporation of Sunderland who at the time were the largest producers of mobile cranes in the world. They bought all types of AEC engines to power Coles Cranes, which were diesel-electric driven in the 10-112 ton capacity range: Neal mobile and truck mounted cranes which were diesel-mechanically driven: Neal-Unit diesel-mechanical excavators: and Taylor Hydra diesel-hydraulic mobile and truck mounted cranes. The B.C. and E.C. exported to over 100 countries world wide, and AEC supplied thousands of engines to them throughout the years. Some AEC powered cranes are still in service. Similarly Newton Chambers and Co. Ltd. of Sheffield used AEC engines in their range of NCK cranes and excavators.

These were also the years of considerable changes in operating conditions. The start of the Motorway age had dawned in 1958 with the opening of a stretch of the M6 by-passing Preston, followed shortly afterwards by a length of the M1 in Northamptonshire. Suddenly engines were being subjected to relatively long periods of flat out running, and whilst the 7.7 litre, 9.6 litre and 11.3 litre engines would run all day at 1,500 rpm, these

engines could knock out big ends if kept at full revs for long periods, due to their crankshafts not being counterbalanced.

AEC were not the only British engine manufacturer to experience these particular problems when Motorway running became more common. The 2AV 590/690 engines had been introduced to cure that particular fault. To withstand long periods of high speed running the 6 speed overdrive gearbox, and higher rear axle ratios were introduced.

Not only were many vehicles having to go faster, some were actually going on longer journeys, with the start of international road haulage operations. For several years unaccompanied trailer movements between Britain and Europe had been taking place, but in the late 1950s a few far sighted and intrepid pioneers started accompanied movements. In May 1954 Whitbread had inaugurated direct deliveries to their Brussels depot from London with Mammoth Major Mk III, LYE 792. Whilst this journey was shorter in mileage than Newcastle is from London, it was a significant and historic event for road transport. John Wyatt Jnr. of Diss, Norfolk, ran the legendary Fridged Freight operation and started direct deliveries to Italy in 1958. It seems hard to believe today that Mammoth Major and Mandator Mk IIIs should go such distances, but they did, and an impressive fleet of Mk V and later tilt cabbed AECs, followed.

John Wyatt and his drivers were true European transport pioneers and they chose AECs to do it with. The gross weights they were running at were well in excess of the vehicle design weights. Then, an insulated refrigerated body was heavy, and as they were also designed for hanging meat transport and all the necessary roof reinforcing for that, the unladen weights alone were awesome. The Mammoth Majors pulled drawbar trailers, mainly built to Wyatt's own specification with AEC axles, and in those days before the Mont Blanc tunnel was constructed and the route was across the punishing Brenner Pass, the Wyatt Fridged Freight AECs were an impressive and memorable sight to behold.

By the end of 1964 over 6,000 Mk Vs had been built, with about half that number being eight wheelers. It shows how much AEC's goods vehicle sales had increased; in comparison it had taken ten years to build a similar number of Mk IIIs, in this same year the BRS general haulage fleet totalled some 7,500 lorries, of which 2,000 were AECs:– 550 Mercury rigids, 500 Mammoth Major eight wheelers, and 950 assorted Mercury and Mandator tractor units. On order from AEC were 400 vehicles for BRS, nearly all of them tractor units. In addition, they operated many AEC engined vehicles, notably Seddons, who supplied a range of tractor units to BRS with AV470, 2AV590, and 2AV690 engines. It was usual for the BRS depots running AECs to operate these Seddons alongside them in the interests of maintenance, and spare parts compatibility.

Also in 1964, Harold Wood had an all-AEC fleet of

over 500 vehicles:– 200 Mammoth Major Mk III eight wheelers, 200 Mammoth Major Mk V eight wheelers, 90 Mandator Mk V tractor units, 10 Monarch Mk III rigids, and 30 assorted Mercury rigids and tractor units. Until 1962 the Harold Wood fleet had been all rigids, but changes were being made on to articulation, and on order from AEC were 72 Mandator tractor units, 16 Mercury tractor units, and 89 Mammoth Major eight wheelers. Of this total, 60 were additional lorries. At that time 50% of the Harold Wood fleet was on contract to large chemical manufacturers, oil companies, and petroleum distributors. To have 577 vehicles ordered by two customers alone in one year indicates how successful the AEC marque had become, and coupled with the numerous orders from other operators large and small, this period would indeed be regarded as the halcyon years for AEC in the light of events only a few years ahead.

Top left: Pioneers of accompanied international transport. This group of drivers and AECs of John Wyatt Jnr. of Diss are photographed in Italy in the mid 1960s. Note the towing bar carried on the front of 1400 PW and the extra fuel tank located above the cab of the Mammoth Major Eight Mk III. (*Chris Wyatt*)

Top left: The registration number of this Mandator Mk V suggests that it did not enter service until 1969, although the last Mk Vs were produced in early 1966. Used for transporting fork lift trucks, it was photographed in Lincolnshire on 4th February 1971. (*Bill Taylor*)

Bottom left: The short wheel base Mammoth Major Eight Mk V pulverised coal tanker contrasts with the background of the Stanton Ironworks. At the time, the National Coal Board were conducting various trials connected with the fluidised discharge of coal, and several AECs were used with a variety of bodies. (*AEC*)

Middle left: Starr Roadways of Bilston operated 789 DNR, a Mammoth Major Six Mk V tractor unit on heavy haulage. Their preference for AECs for this kind of work dated back to when they used a Matador for such tasks. (*Starr Roadways*)

Bottom left: Fred Hope operated many Mandators and Mammoth Majors on abnormal load transport, and this load was typical of his work. He was one of the innovators and great minds of transport, designing and patenting devices and systems aimed at improving heavy goods vehicle safety, including the famous Hope anti-jackknife device for articulated lorries. (*Arthur Ingram*)

Based at Aberlour in the Scottish Highlands, McPhersons operated 'Bonnie Sheila', a Mammoth Major Eight Mk V. The additional AEC logos, horseshoes, and AA badges indicate a well looked after lorry, and most of this company's work was connected with the Scotch whisky industry. (*AEC*)

Top left: Express Dairy ran AECs for decades, and Mammoth Major Eights were favoured for long distance trunking of bulk milk from the collection points to the bottling dairies. The cab on this Mk V is by RTS of Hackney, and as well as twin headlamps, it has front opening 'suicide doors', so called because they were prone to burst open in the event of a collision. (*Arthur Ingram*)

Middle left: Crossing Tower Bridge, one of the many AECs operated by Munro of Aberdeen. Scottish hauliers were very pro-AEC in the 1960s for long distance work, with the Mandator Mk V, such as this one, being favoured. Quality and reliability was very important to them, with lorries which were often working several hundred miles away from home base. (*Arthur Ingram*)

Bottom left: Mammoth Major Six Mk V heavy haulage tractor unit operated by Sunter Bros. of Northallerton. It is coupled up to a 16 wheel skeletal semi-trailer. (*Artur Ingram*)

Left: The Mandator Mk V was available as a short wheelbase heavy duty tipper, and its robust construction made it ideal for such off-road work where road-going payloads could be safely ignored. Here one such example with a scow ended body is loaded, whilst an earlier Mandator Mk III tipper awaits its turn under the Ruston Bucyrus excavator (*Motorphoto*)

Below: Drawbar trailer tanker outfits were never very common, and this Mammoth Major Eight Mk V headed combination makes an interesting sight. The trailer is coupled on a turntable dolly, and in the mid-1960s the legality of such a configuration was questioned, as the counter argument suggested that this, in fact, constituted two trailers being pulled. Clarification in favour of turntable dolly couplings was eventually obtained, and judging by the absence of a second man in the cab, then this photo must date from post-1970, when legislation was passed that made the carrying of a trailer mate no longer necessary. (*Motorphoto*)

Right: The quality of this photograph is not great, but it is included because the Mandator Mk V is one of the 10' 1" wheelbase models, which were not common. It is also one of the last batch of Mk Vs to be built, – chassis no. 3G4RA 3147 – fitted with the AV691 engine, and capable of operating at 32 tons gross train weight. (*Philip Platt*)

Middle left: Captured at Hay Mills, Birmingham, in 1971, one of Billy Smart's Mammoth Major Mk Vs waiting to unload the Big Top seating. At that time, as a result of the introduction of annual testing and plating in 1968, some Mk IIIs and many Mk Vs were finding a further lease of life with fairground showmen and circus proprietors, whose vehicles were exempt from such regulations. (*Bevan Laing*)

Bottom right: On 13th December 1966 this Mammoth Major Six Mk V set off from London for Teheran, the capital of Iran. It arrived there 14 days later, having more than halved the time taken by the existing road-rail service. The payload carried was 24 tons, with the prime-mover carrying a demountable container. The Tillotson built cab was extended to accommodate a sleeping bunk. It was powered by the AV691 engine, and had fitted an up-rated front axle and springs. (*AEC*)

Right: Originally registered in Lancashire, this Stafford based Mandator Mk V was showing a fair turn of speed when captured on the 4th February 1971 in Lincolnshire. (*Bill Taylor*)

Right: One of t[h]e many AEC engine[d] Seddon tract[or] units operated [by] BRS. This is a ty[pe] 30/4/690 dati[ng] from 1965, wi[th] 2AV690 engi[ne] and AEC gearbo[x]. These lorries we[re] let down by the[ir] Moss rear axle[s] which frequent[ly] snapped the ha[lf] shafts. Ted Hann[a] recalls that [he] often attend[ed] such breakdow[ns] on Sha[p] (*Mack [of] Manchester[,] Seddon Atkinso[n]*

Below: The registration number suggests that this Mammoth Major Eight Mk V was previously owned by Harold Wood & Sons Ltd. Berry Wiggins & Co. Ltd. were another well remembered tanker operator. This one was photographed in Lincolnshire on 14th October 1970. (*Bill Taylor*)

eft: Photographed n the site of the rmer Bradford ower station in 979, this is not a ammoth Major x Mk V, but a ype 4G6R4B, hich was a special xed cab 6 x 4 pper chassis vailable between 966-74. They were uilt to a 11 ft. heelbase, with a ouble reduction 2 ering, fully rticulated rear ogie; AV760 ngine with a 6 eed gearbox, and xport size radiator. here was a choice f either a Park oyal Mk V style of ab, or the ropriety Motor anels structure lso used by Guy nd Seddon. In hose not so long go days, when ard hats were not ompulsory, a good ense of balance as also a useful ttribute for a emolition crew. *. Morris Bray*)

Right: This Coles crane was almost certainly destined for the RAF as it is being put through its paces on some soft ground. All such cranes built by the B.C. & E.C. and powered by AEC engines were badged with a yellow triangle motif. (*AEC*)

Right: The natur home of the 18 c yd. capaci Dumptruk was th open cast coal si or large quarr This photograp was taken at th huge open ca coal site Cannock, whe the Dumptruk were subjected t the most intensiv of use. Even whe a driver went for tea break, he wa replaced b another, resultin in them runnin for 24 hours ever day of the wee The excavato deposited 12 ton with ever bucketful; th average load bein four bucketful The AVT110 engines wer subjected t extremes operatin conditions; haulin almost 50 tons coal out of th bottom of the pi up gradients a steep as 1 in and then coastin back down empt (*AEC*

Left: The Turriff construction company operated this AEC powered NCK crane mounted on a chassis built by AWD. Most of the components were Mammoth Major Mk V based, and there is firm evidence that Vickers-Armstrongs of Newcastle-upon-Tyne were involved in the design and production of these mobile cranes. (*AEC*)

Right: Many of the Kent hauliers used what would now be termed as 'cherished registrations', with Alan Firmin no exception. AF 135 was a Mercury with a third axle conversion to 6x2 format. The AEC authorised dealers for Kent, W.H. Gatward Ltd. of Maidstone supplied quite a few Mercurys with the Boys third axle conversion. (*C.V.R.T.C.*)

Left: Carrying a demountable refrigerated container, this somewhat battered Mustang was operated by Eldridge Haulage of Bermondsey. (*Arthur Ingram*)

Below: The tractor takes its trailer load of apples into the packing shed, and Percy Henley's Mercury, I LKK, waits for its load. This was a Boys third axle conversion Mercury, and Jack Henley recalls that "it was a good truck, but terrible in mud or snow". (*Jack Henley*)

Above: The 18 tons gross vehicle weight Mustang found a niche market with several operators who were looking for a little more payload than a four wheeler could legally carry. Laden with empty crates for a Barnsley glass works, this Park Royal cabbed twin steer turns into the works yard to collect another load. (*AEC*)

Left: Tunnel cement were large AEC operators and were probably unique amongst AEC lorry purchasers in having their own design of triangle motif. (Several large AEC bus fleets had their own design of badge fitted). This Mercury is fitted with a Duramin cab with sliding doors. (*C.V.R.T.C.*)

Right: Another memorable Scottish livery was Pollock of Musselburgh, and their new Marshal had been posed outside of the AEC Glasgow depot in 1961. (*AEC/Motorphoto Archive*)

Middle right: Shell-Mex and BP shared a common marketing policy in the 1950s and 60s. This Marshal operated in their fleet and was introduced in the then fairly new yellow and white livery in 1962. (*Arthur Ingram*)

Below: Later Mercury cabs usually had single piece windscreens and this Percy Henley tractor unit, coupled to a 4-in-line semi-trailer sets out with a load of hops. Not many firms ordered custom made radiator blinds such as this; most drivers had to make do with hessian sacks, newspaper, or cardboard, to try and keep warm in winter. (*Jack Henley*)

Right: By 1964, the deep chrome Mercury bumper bar had been replaced by a lighter, aluminium one. Thomas Harwood still maintained his traditional livery, with wooden floor flat platform, tool box, and roof box. This Tillotson cabbed Mercury looks every inch a traditional general haulage lorry. (*Thomas Harwood*)

Below: Scottish Land Development Ltd. handled all home market sales for the AEC Dumptruk range on a sole agency agreement. They supplied other items of plant and operated AECs in their own fleet. Their Mercury is equipped with its own crane for loading and unloading machinery; not a common feature on lorries 30 years ago. (*AEC*)

Top left: The Marshal was never designed for drawbar trailer work, yet Arthur Ingram found this one doing just that. The AV470 engine would certainly have been hard pressed to give a good performance at such train weights (*Arthur Ingram*)

Left: Coward Bros (Haulage) Ltd. was a London firm who also operated a depot at Warrington. Here a well-laden Marshal gives an elderly cyclist a wide berth. Note the severe damage to the nearside of the cab, which would test the skills of the panel beater to the utmost to rectify, as the front scuttle of this cab style was curved in three planes. (*Motorphoto*)

CHAPTER FIVE

MILITARY PROGRESS

The 0853 Matador accomplished all that it was designed for, and much more besides during World War 2. Officially it was described as "the best medium-class tractor in either of the opposed armies". The designer was Charles Cleaver, who had worked for AEC and its pre-cursor from 1909-14. After service in the Great War he had co-founded the Four Wheel Drive Motor Co., and then returned to AEC when they bought that business.

Charles Cleaver also designed and patented the renowned, fully articulated 2 spring rear bogie which was first used on the AEC 6 x 6 War Department chassis, and remained in much the same format on all AEC multi-axle chassis until production ceased in 1977. The majority of Matadors were built as artillery towing tractors, but several were equipped for other tasks, including armoured communications vehicles. Over 400 were built with platform bodies and supplied to the RAF for haulage work with drawbar trailers. These also had basic cabs which could be quickly dismantled. One peculiarity was that the RAF Matadors were fitted with different towing equipment to the army ones, (hooks for the army: jaws and pins for the RAF).

All Matadors intended for towing had 7.9:1 differentials., whilst solo, armoured body types had higher 6.25:1 differentials. For the North African campaign a number were fitted with armoured cabs, platform bodies and a 6-pounder gun, and they became known as 'yellow devils'. Others were equipped with a 440 volt, 65 Kw dynamo which was mounted over, and belt driven from, the gearbox, to provide power for a searchlight.

Whilst Matadors and 6 x 6s operated by the forces did vital work, the general reliability of AECs was recognised by the authorities, and many were entrusted with essential war work. Based at Newbold`s Bakery, Bradford, then one of the five largest bakeries in the country, were some type 0346 Matador tractor units, and in the build up to D-Day, and immediately afterwards, they were used to transport semi-trailer loads of bread to the troops on the South Coast. They worked on a round-the-clock, 7 day week basis.

When the beach-head was established at Normandy, at least 40 Mammoth Majors, — sixes and eights, — and Mammoth Minors, together with their civilian drivers, were commandeered by the War Department and shipped over to France to establish a supply line for the advancing army.

The production of Military vehicles ceased during 1945. One interesting spin off was a specialist 6 x 6 tractor, based upon the type 0854 War Department model. This became type 0858 and 95 were produced between 1945-48 for the Iraq Petroleum Co. Ltd. They were powered by the A205 version of the 9.6 litre engine, driving through a 5 speed mesh gearbox, and 2 speed auxiliary unit. They were a bonneted tractor, and were mostly used for pipeline construction work.

A 'bitsa' AEC put together for some specific task. It is probably the front end of a Mammoth Major Six Mk III grafted onto a White half-track, and it was photographed in a council compound on the outskirts of Sheffield. (*Arthur Ingram*)

Some 0853 Matadors were released immediately after the war through surplus auctions and they were snapped up by all manner of people requiring vehicles with off-road capabilities. Many forestry contractors had recognised the potential of the Matador as a timber tractor, and in 1947 the Douglas Company of Cheltenham sold their first Matador based Douglas timber tractor to R and R. S. Pye of Elmswell, Suffolk. This was a shortened type 0853, re-cabbed with a Mk III style cab, and a larger capacity winch. The first conversions retained the A187 7.7 litre engine, but subsequent models were fitted with the A206 9.6 litre engine.

Increasing international tension, the cold war, and the Korean War led to orders being placed for Military vehicles once again. In 1952 the first AEC Militant Mk Is were delivered to the forces. There were two versions, the 0859 6 x 4, and the 0860 6 x 6: both powered by the A223 version of the 11.3 litre engine. Drive was through a 5 speed constant mesh gearbox and 2 speed auxiliary unit. They were rated as 10 ton cargo carriers by the Army, but were adapted for many roles including 5th wheel tractor units. When production ceased in June 1962, over 3,000 had been produced, including those sold to civilian customers.

In 1953 manufacture of the 0853 Matador was re-started, and almost 1,800 had been built when production finally stopped in 1959. By any standards of comparison the Matador had an exceptionally long service life, and an on-going refurbishment programme in the Army workshops through the years ensured that

when the last ones were released in the 1970s, there were lots of willing buyers for them.

In 1966 the Militant Mk III was announced as the successor to the Mk I. It was specifically developed for the Army, but the RAF took some, and it was also available for general sale to customers at home and abroad. This was a sophisticated and impressive machine, with a cab styled on the recently phased out AEC Mk V heavy goods vehicle range. All Militant Mk IIIs were 6 x 6s, with type 0870 the right hand control version, and type 0880, left hand control. Power was from the AV760 engine rated at 226 bhp at 2,200 rpm, with 618 lb.ft. of torque at 1,500 rpm. Drive was taken through a D203 6 speed overdrive constant mesh main gearbox and unit mounted, 2 speed auxiliary gearbox, (with transfer to the front axle), to the double drive, reduction spiral bevel double helical rear axles. There was a lockable third differential, and the suspension was the fully articulated 2 spring rear bogie. Front wheel drive was available in either low or high range.

Solo, the Militant Mk III was rated at 28 tons gross vehicle weight, with a 56 tons gross train weight. Two wheelbase lengths and a tractor unit option were listed. With the lowest 7.89:1 axle ratio, it had a solo restart ability on a 1 in 3 hill, and at full train weight this was 1 in 7. Top speed of the highest axle ratio version (6.25:1) was 58 mph.

In Army use they served as cargo carriers, tankers, and recovery vehicles, with the latter types having a well equipped inventory made by Scammell, including a

winch, and 4.7 tons capacity slewing crane. Power assisted steering was standard, and the last deliveries were made to the Army in the early 1970s. As they are released from service at the time of writing, they are much sought after as a well equipped heavy recovery vehicle, and good examples fetch high prices at auction.

In addition to the specialist models, large numbers of civilian AECs were supplied to all branches of the forces. 350 Mammoth Major Mk III six wheelers were built at Maudslay for equipping as refuelling bowsers in the early 1950s. Some of the other lorries adapted for various duties over the years were:–

G4R MANDATOR
BLUE STEEL LOAD CARRIER
Based on a half-cab long wheel base Mandator Mk V, they were used to transport the Blue Steel nuclear-armed cruise missiles from storage to the Vulcan and Victor V-bombers which carried them. They were fitted with a special superstructure in the form of davits, with hydraulically powered outriggers to provide stability during loading and unloading operations. These Mandators were based at RAF Scampton and RAF Wittering, and remained in service until 1970. One of them has survived into preservation, and it is on display at the RAF Museum at Hendon.

GM4R MERCURY
2,000 gallon AIR-TRANSPORTABLE REFUELLER
Designed for transportation in RAF Argosy C Mk I,

Beverley, Belfast, and Hercules aircraft, they had a collapsible cab with a detachable fibre-glass hard top. The windscreen could hinge forward, and the steering wheel was removable. The Zwicky Engineering refuelling equipment was also made to a lightweight specification, and the tank, actually of 2,200 gallons capacity, was also of very low height. They were used to dispense all grades of aviation fuels, and out of 52 built, several still survive in use at smaller airfields around the country.

0859 MILITANT
3,500 gallon AIR-TRANSPORTABLE REFUELLER
For use as a prime mover with a 4,500 gallon drawbar trailer tanker, or in solo configuration, these Militant Mk Is were air transportable in Beverley or Belfast aircraft. A variant was adapted to carry the High Test Peroxide fuel used in the Blue Steel missile. This fuel had to be temperature controlled between 15° and 30°C. None of these Militants are now in RAF service, but at least two are operated by B.W.O.C. Ltd.

TG6RB MAMMOTH MAJOR SIX
4,000 gallon ROAD TANKER
These were intended for the transport of fuels overseas, primarily on paved surfaces. They were predominantly used by the RAF at Gutersloh in Germany in a mobile role for the Harrier and support helicopter forces. As at October 1991, 8 of these vehicles dating from 1969-72 were still in service.

TG6RB MAMMOTH MAJOR SIX
HYDROGEN BOTTLE CARRIER

Fitted with a series of compressed gas cylinders, they were used to re-fill balloons used for static drop parachutist training. They usually operated between Cardington, Beds., and Weston-on-the-Green, Oxon. None remain in service today.

TG6RB MAMMOTH MAJOR SIX
DE-ICER

Equipped with a 74' maximum height access platform, they are used to spray de-icing fluid onto large RAF aircraft. The platform and turntable are driven hydraulically from a PTO-driven pump. Four extending hydraulic jacks stabilise the chassis when the platform is in use. Several of these AECs are still in service, and in early 1993, because of defence expenditure cut-backs, investigations had begun to study the feasibility of re-equipping the chassis with new de-icing equipment.

TG6RB MAMMOTH MAJOR SIX
3,000 gallon BOWSER

With re-fueller bodywork and equipment by Gloster

Saro, these bowsers have been the mainstay of the RAF for twenty years. They can handle all types of aircraft fuel and can undertake pressure re-fuelling or de-fuelling, and open line re-fuelling. Equipped with 2½" pressure hoses, they will simultaneously deliver 250 gallons per minute. The Mammoth Majors were procured in three versions, with the Mk I and Mk IA equipped with a two-line braking system.

The final Mk IB model had three-line braking, and more efficient 'Coalescer' fuel filters. All varieties could accept attachments for a snow plough for clearing runways and taxi-ways of snow. They are equipped for towing a 4.500 gallon drawbar trailer weighing, when full, well in excess of 20 tons. The first Mammoth Majors entered service in late 1968, with the final deliveries being in 1977. Many of the earlier vehicles have now been disposed of, with several having gone overseas for further service. They are also sought after by civil airfields, and companies such as Flitwick Ground Support at Rugby, and Flightline at Witney, specialise in re-furbishing them, and converting them to civil aviation specifications. At the time of writing in excess of 100 Mammoth Major bowsers are still in service with the RAF.

Pyes of Elmswell operated 5 Douglas timber tractors. The standard 0853 Matador chassis was shortened, a new cab was fitted, and most of them received the A206 9.6 litre engine. This one is minus its special timber jib in this photograph. The jib and winch controls were air pressure operated. Douglas also supplied the special trailers, known as 'drugs'. BCF 960 survives today in preservation. (*D. MacKenzie collection*)

Several Mammoth Major bowsers had to be flown to Saudi Arabia, and then Turkey, in late 1990 to participate in the Gulf War. With a lower cab height than their replacement, the Leyland Bison and S26 Scammell, they were the only re-fuellers which would fit into the Hercules transport aircraft without any dismantling. They also have a proven track record for operating in hot climates, whereas the other makes have been known to be very temperamental in arduous conditions. The Mammoth Majors served without any problems, and many of them clocked up more mileage in 6 months in Saudi Arabia than they had done in their previous existence, because the aircraft fuel had to be brought some 200 miles to their base at Darhran.

Many Mk III, Mk V and tilt-cab AECs served in the general transport fleet of all branches of the forces, being used for tasks of all kinds between ordnance depots, army camps, naval bases, and airfields. Some of them hardly ever left their bases, such as the Mammoth Major Mk V six wheeler tractor units. They operated at the submarine bases of Coalport and Faslane, and their 2AV690 engines were equipped, in naval fashion, with

waterwash air cleaners and Thornycroft marine-type watercooled manifolds. Mention must also be made of the mysterious TG6RB nuclear war-head carriers. Only eight of these Mammoth Majors were constructed, and they had a much modified and strengthened cab, with a special purpose built body. They came from the very last batch of Mammoth Majors to be built at Southall, and they were only withdrawn from service in the latter part of 1992. The TGM4 Mercury tractor unit was the mainstay of the RAF's general transport fleet for all of the 1970s, and well into the 1980s.

AEC had a great tradition of supplying the armed forces, and even today, in 1994, several AECs are still in service with the Army and RAF, at home and overseas. For quite a while the army workshops undertook a re-furbishment programme of cabs to prolong the working life of the TG models. Some re-fuellers also were re-cabbed entirely with the Leyland T45 Roadtrain cab. Defence expenditure reviews will probably ensure that AECs remain in service for a few years to come. The AEC marque had a life of 67 years: AEC vehicles have already served the armed forces of Britain for 78 years!

Left: The RAF ordered several Matadors when production re-commenced in 1953. This one was based with a signals company and was equipped as a mobile generator. (*Bill Taylor*)

Below: The Militant Mk I was adapted to many roles with the army, and they had a long service life of almost 30 years in some cases. This 6x6 version was photographed at the Spittalgate, Grantham depot on 9th September 1981. (*Bill Taylor*)

Right: Long wheelbase Mandator Mk Vs were adapted by the RAF as transfer carriers for the Blue Steel cruise missile. This photograph, taken of such a vehicle on display at RAF Wittering shows the missile swung out on its davits, and the support stabilisers can just be made out. One of these Mandators is on public display at the RAF Museum, Hendon. (*Bill Taylor*)

Right: Based on a 2GM4RA Mercury chassis; the air-transportable 2,000 gallon re-fueller. By dismantling the top half of the rudimentary cab and removing the steering wheel, then a uniform height was possible. Konsin is a very expensive de-icing fluid. (*Bill Taylor*)

Top left: An impressive line up of Mandator Mk V re-fuellers at the Yeovilton base of the Royal Navy. Photographed on 22nd October 1977, also clearly visible is a Mammoth Major Six Mk III re-fueller, which would have been 25 years old at the time. (*Bill Taylor*)

Below right: The work-horse of the RAF's transport fleet from the 1960s until the mid 1980s was the Mercury tractor unit, and they hauled a variety of trailers with a multitude of loads. This one, with a low-loader semi-trailer, was photographed on 18th May 1978. (*Bill Taylor*)

Left: As opposed to the airfield based Mammoth Major Six re-fuellers, this is one of the road going tankers intended for transporting fuel abroad in support of Harrier and Helicopter forces. Still in service in Germany in late 1991, the run-down of British forces there could see the remaining tankers being sold at auction in the near future. (*AEC*)

Above: The RAF also operated a sizeable fleet of Mammoth Major Six load carriers. They had a 24' body with detachable drop-sides, and were intended for transporting palletised loads, spares and supplies, or a standard 20' ISO container. They were also entrusted with transferring Bloodhound missiles around; such a load is being carried on the drawbar trailer of this one. The style of the front grille panel would suggest that it dates from 1974-5; one of the last load carriers to be supplied to the RAF. (*Bill Taylor*)

Left: Arriving at No. 431 Maintenance Unit of RAF Germany, a Mercury with a 'Queen Mary' semi-trailer, on which is a vintage aircraft. (*Bill Taylor*)

Below: For normal duties RAF vehicles were painted in dull finish, with all chrome and brightwork also covered. Special display units, however, received a special paint job, with all chrome highly polished. This Mercury had received the full treatment when photographed at Middle Wallop on 24th July 1982. (*Bill Taylor*)

Top right: One of the Mammoth major Six de-icers, which, at the time of writing, will continue in service for several years to come. The platform will extend to a height of 74', to enable the largest of RAF aircraft to be sprayed with de-icing fluid before taking off. These AECs weigh 23.285 tonnes. (*Bill Taylor*)

Middle right: The Mammoth Major Six 3,000 gallon re-fuelling bowser has been the mainstay of the RAF for over 20 years. This one is coupled to a Tecalemit/Zwicky drawbar trailer of 4,500 gallons capacity. In solo configuration the laden weight is 25.647 tonnes, and with the trailer the gross train weight is just over 46 tonnes. (*Bill Taylor*)

Bottom right: One of the 0859 Militant Mk I 6x4 air transportable re-fuellers, formerly in service with the RAF, and now operated by B.W.O.C. at North Weald airfield. Photographed in May 1989. (*Brian Goulding*)

Left: Bought from Army service principally for its winching capability, this 0870 Militant Mk III operates in the heavy recovery business of F. Ratcliffe & Son, of Conington, Peterborough. A considerable amount of weight reduction was carried out before it was deemed entirely suitable for civilian use. (*Author*)

Below: The Harris family still uses Matadors in fairground service, with two of these three now having AV470 engines in place of the A187 7.7 litre unit. WPX still carries a very original early style of Matador cab. Photographed at Ardingly in July 1992. (*Author*)

AEC In Colour

The majority of the photographs used in this colour section have been provided by Peter Davies, one of our foremost lorry photographers, whose contribution to the post-war history and recording of Britain's road transport industry is invaluable. The author is deeply grateful for the use of these photographs.

Right: In service with H. Tideswell &Sons Ltd., based at Kingsley near Stoke on Trent, this 1959 Mammoth Major 6 Mk III milk tanker was photographed at their depot on 24th October 1968. It has a lightweight aluminium Duramin cab. *(Peter Davies)*

Above: When photographed on 3rd October 1968 at Starch Products Ltd. Slough factory, this Mammoth Major 8 Mk III was still looking to be in good condition at 17 years old. The introduction of annual testing and plating in that year rapidly brought about the demise of many splendid old work horses such as this, as it was uneconomic to uprate the braking systems of lorries of this age to comply with the new legal requirements. *(Peter Davies)*

Top right: This Mammoth Major 6 Mk III re-fueller was supplied to the Royal Naval Air Service base at Yeovilton, and was one of an order placed by the War Office in 1951. Because these were non-standard Mammoth Majors, they were built at Maudslay's Parkside Works at Coventry. When photographed in 1984, this was one of three still in service, but at the end of the year they had all been withdrawn. Several of these AECs have survived into preservation, and usually a flat platform body has replaced the tank and re-fuelling booms. (*Robin Pearson*)

Middle left: Just as van operators in Yorkshire designed their van bodies to take local needs into account, then the raw wool hauliers used to build extensions over the cabs to carry extra bales of wool. Chris Metcalfe Ltd., based at Keighley operated this 1961 Park Royal cabbed Mercury Mk II, and it was captured on film in Luton on 28th June 1970. (*Peter Davies*)

Left: Allied Industrial Services of Bradford operated this Luton van bodied Mustang, supplied in 1959. Note that it has a canvas sheet in place of a solid roof, to facilitate overhead loading from the upper floors of multi-storey premises. This style of van roof was very popular with many operators in the woollen towns of Yorkshire. Photographed on 17th August 1968. (*Peter Davies*)

Right: A wet quayside, and a 1964 Park Royal cabbed Marshal collects a load of pulp, probably destined for one of the Medway towns paper mills. (*Author's collection*)

Right: Typical of the huge number of Mercury articulated outfits operated by BRS in the 1960s. This 1962 8ft wheelbase version, rated for 18 tons gross vehicle weight operations, was based in the Nottingham area. It was photographed on the North Circular Road at Ealing on 9th September 1968. (*Peter Davies*)

Below: Tunnel Cement were in the 'first division' of loyal operators, and they purchased over 800 AECs between 1935-1977. This 1962 Mammoth Major Mk V, with a Duramin cab, has a double bubble powder tank, designed and built by Interconsult. It was captured on film on a wet Glasgow day at Tunnel Cement's Clydebank works on 29th October 1968. *(Peter Davies)*

Left: Mk Vs without a bumper bar always looked 'unfinished'. Here one of the large Allisons' fleet of Mandators has just loaded with rolls of jute, and the driver is securing his load in the correct manner: 'sheet from the rear, rope from the front'. Allisons were based in Dundee, with a London depot, and faded from the transport scene in the early 1970s. *(AEC)*

Right:
A. & R.J. Wood of Sittingbourne operated this Mammoth Major Eight Mk V, seen here with a load of picket fencing. Their livery of black chassis, royal blue, and light blue cab suited the Mk V very well, and combined to present a traditional British haulage lorry at it's best. (*Author's collection via M. Clancy*)

Right: With low-loader semi-trailer and Ruston Bucyrus 22-RB excavator, the Greenham Mandator Mk V would have been operating nearer to its 36 tons gross train design weight, rather than the normal 24 tons limit applied to general haulage lorries. Photographed in October 1963, the loading appears to be spot on, giving a perfectly balanced outfit. (*AEC*)

Right: Heading through the Orange Free State in South Africa in 1965, A Mammoth Major Six Mk V bitumen spreader/tanker, and drawbar trailer. Operated by Tanker Services, it was running at a gross train weight of 40 tons. (*AEC*)

Left: Another large Yorkshire haulier whose lorries were often seen with huge woollen bale loads was Henry Long Ltd. of Manningham, Bradford. Photographed at its home base on 10th August 1973, this 1960 Mandator Mk V tractor unit had then completed 13 years of service. Although conceived when 24 tons gross vehicle weight was the legal maximum for the appropriate class of lorry, only minor modifications were required to uprate Mandator Mk Vs to either 30 or 32 tons gross vehicle weight specification, as introduced in the Construction and Use Regulations of 1965. (*Peter Davies*)

Below right: When photographed on 27th June 1967 at Roxton, near St. Neots, this 0853 Matador 4 x 4 still carried an original style of cab. Operated by Fensoms of Colmworth as a winching vehicle, it had been registered for highway use in 1952, which was the year in which many Matadors were sold off as surplus to requirements, by the War Office. Co-incidentally, production of this all time classic AEC was just about to recommence at Southall. (*Peter Davies*)

Right: From the mid-1980s, large numbers of Militant Mk Is became available through Government surplus dealers, and this 6 x 6 version was seen in 1989 at L.W. Vass Ltd., Ampthill, one of the largest dealers in ex-MOD AECs. (*Peter Davies*)

Below: Whilst the 18 cu. yd. capacity Dumptruk was not entirely successful in service, the smaller 10 cu. yd. capacity 690 version was a very popular model, with many of them surviving 15-20 years of arduous service. Manufacture was transferred from Southall to Aveling-Barford, with the final LD-55 version being built by Scammell. At least two 690s are known to be still operating in 1993. (*AEC*)

Above: Spiers of Melksham will always be associated with their fleet of AEC Mandator tractor units which soldiered on into the late 1980s, but they were committed AEC users, of many different types, for many years before they became a 100% articulated fleet. Here one of their Mercurys is captured on film well laden with a load of sawn timber. In the background is the cab of an earlier Mercury or Marshal.
(Author's collection via M. Clancy)

Left: The 15' wheelbase Mercury could be bodied as a tipper, tanker or flat platform. S. Billitt & Son of March operated this Murfitt bodied one, and with the tipper body sides folded down, it could then serve as a flat lorry for carrying sacks of corn or fertiliser. *(AEC)*

Below: Express Dairy, another long standing AEC operator, used several Mercurys for inter-depot trunking duties, and this 1973 tractor unit and single axle semi-trailer was photographed at Ruislip on 2nd July 1974, when it was less than 12 months old.
(Peter Davies)

Right: Photographed when new, the driver of this Distillers Co. Mercury tractor unit and liquid carbon dioxide tanker semi-trailer was taking part in the Lorry Driver of the Year competition, held at Bramcote on 9th September 1973. (*Peter Davies*)

Middle left: Just loaded with hot tarmacadam at Mountsorrell Quarry, Leicestershire on 4th December 1967 Redland Gravel's Marshal could legally carry a 14 tons payload within its 22 tons gross vehicle weight limit. The recently introduced tilt-cab, and premium specification of both the Mercury and Marshal ranges, set these popular medium weights a class apart from their competition, and this was reflected in the booming sales figures for AEC in the mid-1960s. (*Peter Davies*)

Below: The long wheel base 6x4 Marshal was always a popular lorry with livestock hauliers, and this one with a sapele mahogany body made by Tiverton Coachbuilders, could carry up to 24 cows, or 60 pigs, or 80 sheep. Presumably the upper front panel of the body could be easily removed to allow the cab to be tilted. (*AEC*)

Right: Mercury drawbar trailer combinations were not very common, but several operators did run them for specialist applications, such as the one shown here. The maximum legal gross train weight for a Mercury and trailer was 26 tons. Stephensons of Huddersfield were part of the Austin Hall Group, and this photograph was taken on 24th April 1974 at Toddington Services on the M1 Motorway. *(Peter Davies)*

Right: Alongside a compound of TK Bedfords, this smart blue and yellow liveried Marshal waste disposal tanker was photographed on 18th June 1969. The location was Windmill Road, Luton. *(Peter Davies)*

Right: In 1971, Theodore Emms of Dudley, steel stockholders, parked up their fleet of lorries because of a prolonged industrial relations dispute. After some 17 years under cover, six AECs were bought, and some of these were put back into service. This Marshal was one of them, and it was operated by A. & R. Davies of Kingswinford, on contract to Genner Iron and Steel. (*Peter Davies*)

Right: R.F. Morrison of Rotorua in the North Island of New Zealand operated this 1966-67 Mammoth Major Eight on round timber haulage. Far more AEC buses than AEC lorries were sold there over the years. (*AEC*)

Left: Not many Marshal 8s were built, and even fewer survived in service until the late 1970s. Robert Woodcock of Ampthill ran this most rare flat platform version, seen here delivering its load of bricks to a new housing development at Chandos Road, Ampthill. (*Peter Davies*)

Right: Although badged as a Marshal, WYB 153M is in fact a Marshal Major, and on 26th August 1991 it was hard at work on a Cambridgeshire farm hauling grain. It had just returned to work after being laid up in 1982, when it had been dry-stored with a view to preservation. (*Author*)

Right: Taken at rest at Toddington Services on 18th July 1974, a 1970 Mammoth Major 8 in the livery of Tar Distillers Ltd. The AEC was a contract vehicle supplied by Harold Wood & Sons Ltd., and this large and famous tanker operator was by that date an autonomous division within the Pickfords organisation. (*Peter Davies*)

Right: A 1975 Mammoth Major 8 tar boiler tanker used by BRE on road re-surfacing work. The location is the junction of the A1/A507 at Clophill, Beds., when the A1 was being re-surfaced. (*Peter Davies*)

Right: Assembled at Dundalk, Ireland, this 1968 Mandator was photographed prior to entering service with Chas. Dougherty & Co. Ltd. It is interesting to note that the offside cab step is enclosed, something never seen on Southall built tilt-cab AECs. (*Fotorama of Dundalk, for AEC*)

Right: In May 1973 the annual Tipcon exhibition took place at Blackpool, and this Mammoth Major 8 demonstrator was on show there. (*Peter Davies*)

Left: Because cement is a very dense substance, it is possible to obtain maximum weight loads with a relatively small tank, and the short wheelbase eight wheeler has always been a popular choice for such loads. This Pitstone based Mammoth Major was photographed on 22nd June 1973 at Perivale. (*Peter Davies*)

Below: The first AECs to receive the new tilt-cab were Mandators and Mercurys. This AV691 engined Mandator had been recently delivered to McVeigh Transport of Grimsby in 1965, when it was posed on a dockside for a memorable photograph. (*AEC*)

Left: The 'J' registration, Leyland grille badge and hub logos, date this Mammoth Minor from late 1970, and it was only a few months old when photographed in the spring of 1971 on the A17 at Fosdyke. Such configurations were no longer necessary to achieve the maximum 32 tons gross train weight, except with relatively short tipping trailers such as this. The twin steer tractor unit was not to regain popularity until 1983, when an increase in weight limits caused them to be sold once again. (*Bill Taylor*)

Left: The Apple Growers Association Ltd. of Kent operated this impressive Mandator and drawbar trailer on cross-channel and domestic journeys. Photographed on a wet summer day, the blue and red livery highlights the attractiveness of a tilt-cab AEC. (*AEC*)

CHAPTER SIX

AEC OVERSEAS

66 I watched the formative years of AEC from a distance and grew up to recognise the vehicles which emerged from the company's factory as thoroughbreds. At that time, even in the wildest journeyings of my imagination, I did not foresee myself as a leader of the team producing the present world famous vehicles. Since those early days the team and its products have multiplied many times until today they occupy a position of respect as leaders of the industry. But even more important in this fast shrinking world of 1962 is the resounding impact the company has made on world markets. The measure of this development may be gauged from the fact that almost half the current output is shipped overseas. Growth in world markets has received immense stimulus in recent years. Prospects for the future will be closely allied to the pattern of economic development in Europe, where the company has already established itself in preparation for renewed expansion."

These foregoing words were written by Sir William (Bill) Black, then the Chairman of AEC Ltd., in the foreword of a Jubilee Year edition of the 'AEC Gazette' in 1962. They are reproduced here because they sum up perfectly the relevance of exports to AEC, and having established an important world wide market, they saw Europe as an important region of potential growth. It is almost with incredulity that when we look back 30 years and realise that the then level of exports not only enjoyed by AEC, but by all the other major British vehicle manufacturers now no longer exists, then we must wonder why such a situation was ever allowed to happen.

To catalogue all the countries where AEC exported to would require more than this one chapter, but the first overseas sales commenced during the 1920s, and grew steadily in the years before the second World War. After the War, the Government decreed that all manufacturing industry should direct at least 60% of production to the export drive, and it was during this period when AEC really started to capitalise on the contacts they had previously established, not only in the former British Empire, but also in territories such as South America. The models exported were based on the domestic market types, but were available as either left or right hand control, and as normal control bonneted lorries for countries which preferred that configuration. Normally they retained the same model names, but the Mercury range was badged as Monarchs to pacify the Ford Motor Company whose Mercury car was sold world wide. Since the early 1930s AECs sold in South America had been badged ACLO, after an objection by the German owned electrical equipment manufacturer, AEG. Some specific AEC export models were produced and they will be described later.

There can be no doubt that AEC's successes overseas were due to a competitive vehicle range, sold

by a dedicated, specialist, and enthusiastic export department, with salesmen receiving solid technical support from field service engineers, and Southall based personnel. Many of these people were fluent in the languages of the countries where they operated, and some of them lived in the regions for many years. From the late 1940s territories were gradually expanded to cover the Middle East, West Africa, South East Asia, and Europe, as well as greatly increasing sales in South Africa and Australia. Much of this expansion came from the setting up of joint ventures with local concerns to assemble knocked down chassis kits (CKD). There were some 19 countries where associated AEC companies, subsidiaries, joint ventures, or CKD operations thrived. In addition there were further dealer or distribution representations in over 60 countries. Sometimes the main outlet in a particular market would be for AEC buses, but in the majority, buses and lorries were sold side by side.

Australia was one of AEC's first foreign markets,

and sales had grown until by 1964 over 600 lorry chassis a year were being exported. By the nature of the terrain and the huge distances covered, many of the heavyweight models went to work there. Mammoth Major Mk V and the tilt cab lorries were supplied as both six and eight wheeler tractor units. Also popular was the Majestic bonneted six wheeler, one of the AECs specifically designed for overseas. With a rated gross vehicle weight of 25 tons and a gross train weight of 56 tons, they were available in a choice of two wheelbases. Designated as type GB6L or R they were sold from 1958 until 1968, and were initially fitted with the 2AV690 engine. Later ones received the AV760 engine rated at 226 bhp at 2,200 rpm. Drive was via the D203 6 speed overdrive constant mesh gearbox, and double drive, double reduction spiral bevel double helical axles, with the tough fully articulated 2 spring rear bogie suspension. A 2 speed auxiliary gearbox was optional.

A four wheel bonneted load carrier or tractor unit, the Mogul, type GB4L or R complimented the Majestic,

The scene outside the workshops of AEC Australia, with a new Hastings Deerings sleeper cabbed Mandator tractor unit, a new 15' wheel-base Mandator, a Marshal six wheeler, and another new Mandator tractor unit. Note the 'hand on a stick' temporary direction indicators on the doors of the first two Mandators. (AEC)

"Here is my cab, the load is some way behind." The Lennox Heavy Transport and Erection Co. Pty. Ltd. of Sydney operated this long wheel base Mammoth Major Six Mk III, with a tandem axle dolly, and tri-axle low loader. When photographed in 1962 it had just transported the 41½ tons Lima 1201 shovel from Woolloomooloo across the Blue Mountains to Lithgow. (*AEC*)

and was rated at 16 tons gross vehicle weight, and 32 tons gross train weight. It was available as a 13' 4½" wheelbase rigid or tractor unit, as well as a 19' 7" wheelbase load carrier. The specification was identical to the six wheeler except for the rear end, which was the single extra heavy duty double reduction axle. Both chassis were available with either right or left hand control. Certain of the other lorry range showed subtle variations from their home market AEC counterparts, for instance the domestic 2GM4 Mercury became the Monarch Mk VI, and as type 3GM4 was available in four wheelbase lengths with an optional Eaton 2 speed axle. AEC (Australia) Pty. Ltd. had been established in association with Hastings Deering Pty. Ltd. with headquarters in Sydney, and representation in all the other large Australian cities.

South Africa became an important AEC outlet with agreement being forged with J.H. Plane, Africa Ltd. This was AEC's first overseas manufacturing venture and led to the formation of two companies in 1959 based on a Johannesburg plant. AEC Vehicles (SA) Ltd., handled manufacture and sales in South Africa, whilst AEC Central Africa (Pvt) Ltd., dealt with markets such as Rhodesia (Zimbabwe) and neighbouring countries. So

successful were these ventures that after just over one year's trading, sales were reported to have increased by 700%! All types of AECs operated there including one or two special models. The AEC Super Mammoth was an impressive, bonneted six wheel tractor unit powered by the AVT1100 engine. Also specially designed for South Africa was the AEC Kudu bus, but with a chassis layout more akin to a lorry, in that the 2AV690 engine was mounted at the front, to be relatively immune from the dust and mud. Introduced in 1960, some of these Kudus were known to be still in service in 1992.

In South America the main markets were in Argentina, Uruguay, and Peru. During 1961 an agreement for CKD assembly of buses and lorries was signed with Siam di Tella Automores S.A. of Buenos Aires, and this immediately resulted in new orders for over 1,000 vehicles, valued then at £4.6 million. Peru provided some extremely hostile and challenging terrain, with some of the Andes passes reaching altitudes of 16,000 ft. and journeys of up to 1,500 miles, much of which was along unmade roads. To compensate for the serious power losses in the rarefied mountain atmosphere, AEC supplied Moguls and Majestics with their 2AV690 engines in turbo-charged format. Also sold

This 2G4R Mandator Mk V 'A train' in South Africa is of sufficient interest alone, but it is also being loaded by a Coles crane powered by an AEC 11.3 litre engine. The locally made cab has a sleeper extension, but the mirrors are ridiculously small for an outfit with an overall length of some 80 feet. (*AEC*)

in Peru were AEC industrial and marine engines, and these were reported to run for at least twice the number of hours as comparative engines before requiring overhaul. It is quite probable that several AECs are still operating in these South American countries.

Sales in the Middle East region were mainly handled by companies within the Mitchell Cotts Group, and whilst most of the business obtained was for buses, some interesting specialist lorry orders were won. By the early 1960s there were at least 500 AEC Matador and Militant Mk Is at work in the oilfields, where their all wheel drive capability was invaluable. Also specifically designed for trans-desert work was a bus built on a Mammoth Major Mk V six wheeler chassis. These 6 x 4 vehicles were equipped with a 48 seater Jonckheere body and covered a route from Maheila Road to Karima for Sudan Railways.

Nearer to home the late 1950s saw AEC opening up markets on mainland Europe, and established in Ireland was a CKD assembly operation at the Dundalk works of Commercial Road Vehicles. Portugal had long been established as an important outlet, and although a country of low population, AEC obtained about 20% of total lorry sales there for many years, and most of the bus business. In 1961 agreement was reached with Uniaco de Transportadores para Importacao e Comericio Limitasa of Lisbon, thankfully known as U.T.I.C. which had been established as a limited liability partnership in 1944. It consisted of 85% of all the bus and transport undertakings in Portugal, and had been formed originally to import and supply commercial vehicles. Now it was to assemble five CKD chassis per week and manufacture either its own bus bodies or lorry cabs. U.T.I.C. continued to take AEC chassis until the last days of Southall. Another important Portuguese customer was the State Railway company, which bought turbo-charged AH 11.3 litre engines for their railcars.

In Finland, Vanajan Autohedes used AEC engines, gearboxes, and rear axles in their range of Vanajan lorries. The year 1961 saw AEC investing in Barreiros of Madrid, Spain, and Barreiros-AEC S.S. built AECs under licence, and in addition to which Barreiros used AEC engines in most of its range of lorries and buses. Ironically, when this company exported 'Spanish Dodge' tractor units to Britain in the late 1970s for a few years, they received acclaim for their engines which were based on, and directly descended from the AEC 2AV590/690 units. In 1962 AEC reached agreement with O.M.T. of Tortona in Italy to supply them with 2AV690 engines for use in the first Italian purpose built eight wheelers. Rated at 22 tons gross vehicle weight and 44 tons gross train weight, these rigid eights had an air suspended, self steering fourth axle.

Amongst the most exciting agreements, with lots of future potential was the one reached with

Above: What was then Rhodesia, and is now Zimbabwe, was a large user of AECs, and some are still believed to be operating at the time of writing. Smith & Youngson Ltd. of Salisbury ran this Mammoth Major Eight Mk V on refrigerated transport. Surprisingly, the second front axle is un-braked. (*AEC*)

Top right: An interesting Mammoth Major Eight Mk V operating in South Africa. The cab is similar to the British RTS build, with front opening doors. The driver has a tiny mirror on his side, and none at all on the nearside. The straight through exhaust system is of generous proportions and no doubt sounded very throaty. A container of water is hanging from the offside towing eye. (*AEC*)

Etablissements Willeme of Nanterre, France. It started in 1958 with AEC supplying AV470 and AV690 engines because Willeme were not satisfied with their existing units. This led on to AEC investing money, and by 1964 Willeme was quite a large operation, producing some 2,000 chassis annually with AEC engines, and in the case of their K301, AV470 powered four wheeler model, an AEC rear axle also. Eventually the AV 691/760 engine was supplied, and whilst badged as Willeme, the front grilles of the cabs were distinctly AEC Mk V style and featured the blue triangle motif. They established some 50 sales and service points in France and North Africa, and when the agreement was terminated in late 1967, Willeme went out of business shortly afterwards.

Scandinavia was not a large market for AEC, but some important business was obtained there, with a small CKD operation being established in Norway. Denmark took many AECs through the years: amongst them Dumptruks and several sleeper cabbed Mandator Mk IIIs, used on the trans-European transport of fish and frozen foods. AEC made financial investments in N.V. Auto Industrie Vereul in Holland who built buses with AEC running units, and also the Stokvis Group imported Mandator and Mammoth Major Mk V chassis and fitted them with a locally built cab. They also marketed a range of AEC industrial engines, and the railcars of Dutch Railways were powered by the AH1100

engine. The Delft company A. de Boo N.V., operated a sizeable fleet of Monarchs on construction projects.

Quite a large operation was established in Belgium, and this grew out of the dealership founded in 1949 by Etablissements Guy Spitals to import AEC and Maudslay vehicles. In 1960 the company was re-named as AEC Continental. Not only did they sell AECs of all types, they also organised the basis for a European service network in conjunction with operators in other Benelux countries. The Mandators and Mammoth Majors sold by them from 1962 were fitted with an attractive all-steel cab manufactured by Ateliers Bollekens S.A., and these cabs would certainly not have looked out of place on AECs travelling along British roads.

Many AEC 6 x 4 Marshals and 10 cu.yd. Dumptruks served the construction industry of Greece for many years, and the islands of Cyprus and Malta relied almost exclusively on AECs for their heavy transport requirements for decades. Nowadays, the AECs of Malta are mainly imported second hand models, and to a Maltese driver a 24 ton rating of a Marshal means 24 tons of payload! However, they keep going, and the kind climate ensures that the tilt-cabs last longer than they ever did in Britain.

By any yardstick, AECs achievements in world markets were impressive, and they truly were an internationally acclaimed make of lorry, engendering a deep respect, which in many places where they operated, is still retained to this day.

Top left: The Super Mammoth was a massive tractor unit powered by the AVT1100 engine rated at 300 bhp. They mainly operated in South Africa and Zimbabwe (Rhodesia). (*AEC*)

Middle left: This Matador (4x2) tractor unit was one of the first of the AECs to be imported into Belgium by G. Spitals in 1949. It has a locally built cab and it is coupled to a Daf 4-in-line step frame semi-trailer. At that time Daf had yet to produce their first lorry. (*F. Van De Plas/ F. Ceulemans*)

eft: Photographed eaving Windmill Lane, Southall in 1963 is ACLO Mogul tractor unit, chassis number GB4RA 346, probably heading for the docks for shipping to Peru. AEC)

Bottom left: With a locally built cab, a Mammoth Major Mk III six wheel tractor unit of the Belgian Van Twist company. (*Motorphoto/ AEC archive*)

Left: A 1960 Mammoth Major Six Mk III operated by the Brewery Lamot in Belgium. The cab was locally made by Altiers Bollekens. (*F. Van De Plas/ AEC Continental*)

Top left: S.A.M.S.S. of Antwerp operated this sleeper cabbed Mogul on trans-European haulage, seen here coupled to a rather short Monks refrigerated semi-trailer, which has an under mounted 'fridge unit'. (*Motorphoto/ AEC archive*)

Middle left: This Mandator tipper is still in service in Belgium at the time of writing. It is a TG4L chassis with a Bollekens cab, which appears to be a temporary store for a stack of plastic bread baskets. (*F. Van De Plas/ Gebr. Van Loon*)

Left: A Mammoth Major Six Mk V tipper with a Bollekens cab from 1963-64. This lorry was based near Antwerp. The full width, all-steel cabs were much roomier than their British Mk V counterparts. (*AEC*)

Bottom left: Willeme produced a range of rigid and articulated lorries with AEC engines. This is their RD201 6 wheeler, rated at 26 tonnes gross vehicle weight. It was powered by the AV690 engine, with a ZF 12 speed gearbox. Some other models were virtually AECs, with all the main components supplied by Southall. (*Arthur Ingram*)

Right: AECs were assembled at Dundalk in Ireland, and useful levels of sales were established there. This Mandator Mk V is fitted with a cab, built locally by Tommy McArdle, who was supplied with drawings, somewhat reluctantly, by Park Royal Vehicles. (*C.V.R.T.C.*)

Below: With a locally built cab, a Monarch belonging to A. De Boo of Delft discharges a load of ready mixed concrete. Note the position of the windscreen wipers. (*AEC*

Right: This left hand control Marshal was probably assembled by UTIC in Lisbon between 1965-67. Most of the overseas markets preferred the split windscreen version of the Sankey tilt-cab; an option available in Britain but rarely specified. (*AEC*)

Below: The Dutch company of A.G. Burgler used this Mogul as a prime mover, with a large capacity drawbar tank trailer, on milk haulage. (*AEC*)

Top left: Built in 1969, the cab on this Mammoth Major Six tractor unit was still in outstanding condition when photographed in 1990. It is operated by Kevin Power, a grain and sunflower seed farmer in Bowenville, Western Australia. He also owns a Mammoth Minor, a GM6 Marshal, and one of the rare 4GM4RA Matador Mk II 4x4 vehicles. (*Kevin Power*)

Middle left: Still soldiering on at nearly 30 years old, a GM6 Marshal towing its own fork lift truck in Malta, July 1990. (*Craig Temple*)

Bottom left: This UTIC cabbed Mammoth Major Six Mk V was still in service in Lisbon in April 1989. It is just possible to see the UTIC triangle motif, which differed from the AEC one. (*Arthur Ingram*)

Right: Liberally coated with dust, this long wheel base Mammoth Major Six tipper ops up with diesel in readiness for more hard work. Malta, July 1990 (*Craig Temple*)

Below: Unmistakably Malta, with a Marshal 6x4 tipper as the centrepiece. It is very probable that the mobile crane is AEC powered as well. Photographed on 16th July 1990. (*Craig Temple*)

The island of Cyprus still has plenty of AECs in service, with the Lefkaritis company operating a variety. They have many hundreds of abandoned lorries 'in store' on the island. This Mercury tanker was photographed in February 1993. (*Brian Goulding*)

CHAPTER SEVEN

THE FINAL YEARS 1965~1979

The Golden Years for AEC did not suddenly come to an end in 1964, because as a result of the introduction of a new, tilt-cab goods vehicle range at the Commercial Motor Show in that year, sales continued to increase for a few more years. There are many influences and considerations to be taken into account when reviewing this period, the final years of AEC, so it is perhaps necessary to sub-divide this chapter into the relevant areas of legislation, vehicles, and company policy, to hopefully give a coherent account of the events which terminated with the closure of Southall.

LEGISLATION

The 1960s produced much legislation concerned with commercial vehicles. This obviously was to have a direct influence on AEC's policy regarding its new range. The 1964 Construction and Use Regulations increased the permissible weight limits for goods vehicles and allowed them to become longer and wider. The same regulations also applied to lorries registered on or after 1st February 1963, and if they had been 'plated' to operate at the new, higher, weight limits by the manufacturer, then they could do so. Under the new C. and U. Regulations all rigid vehicles could be up to a maximum of 36' long and 8' 2" wide. Maximum permissible gross weights were:– for a four wheeler, 16 tons: for a six wheeler, 22 tons: and for an eight wheeler, 28 tons, but

it was not that straightforward. A six wheeler with under 18' outer axle spread was limited to a maximum of 20 tons gross weight, and for an eight wheeler to qualify for the full 28 tons rating it had to have a minimum 26' outer axle spread, which made them unwieldy and awkward to manoeuvre. Consequently, most were built with shorter wheelbases to run at either 24 tons or 26 tons gross vehicle weights. Any rigid lorry pulling a drawbar trailer could gross up to 32 tons.

The articulated vehicle maximum gross train weight limit was raised to 32 tons and for the first time there was a distinct payload advantage over an eight wheeler. Even though a rigid and drawbar trailer combination could match the payload of an articulated tractor and semi-trailer, the former outfit still had to carry a trailer mate, which was an additional cost, (this law was relaxed in 1970). The increase in gross train weights hastened the move to articulation even more. These new articulated vehicle regulations were rather complex in relation to gross weights and outer axle spreads. The maximum overall vehicle length could be 42' 8", an increase of some 7', and this allowed a semi-trailer length of up to 33'. A gross train weight of 32 tons was possible with a 5 axle combination and 32' outer axle spread, but this was reduced to 30 tons with a 4 axle outfit. To qualify for the maximum 32 tons on four axles only, required an outer axle spread of 38', which was almost impossible to achieve within the overall length limit. Where this was accomplished then

the rear axles had to be located at the extreme rear of the semi-trailer, which not only made manoeuvering awkward, but also caused problems with correct axle weight loadings. To provide a solution to these difficulties the Mammoth Minor twin steer tractor was introduced in 1965.

The Mandator tractor unit coupled to a 33' tri-axle flat platform, semi-trailer could qualify for the maximum gross train weight loading, and typically the payload would be about 22 tons. The start of containerisation in the seaports at this time resulted in ISO standard containers being introduced, and this in turn led to the overall articulated vehicle length bring increased to 48' 9" in 1968, allowing a semi-trailer length of 39'. This amendment made tractor units such as the Mammoth Minor no longer necessary.

The 1964 C. and U. Regulations also laid down minimum braking standards for all vehicles, and tractor units had to be equipped with separate circuits for tractor and trailer service brakes operated through a dual foot control valve. A power assisted parking brake

operating the tractor driving axle brakes was required, and a separate emergency brake, to operate on the tractor front axle and semi-trailer axle or axles, through a third line was also required. To meet these new regulations multiple diaphragm brake chambers were fitted.

In 1968 the annual testing and plating of all goods vehicles became a statutory requirement, with minimum braking standards to be met. Under the provisions of this act it was compulsory for all vehicles operating after 1972 to be equipped with dual braking systems. AEC issued bulletins and provided conversion kits for all their vehicles built from 1958 to be uprated to meet the new requirements if operators wished to do so. The effect of annual testing and plating was to remove many older vehicles from the roads because it was not economically viable to uprate them to new standards. Some Mammoth Major Mk III and older Mk V eight wheelers were converted to four axle braking, and some continued to operate with three axle braking but at lower plated gross weights. Generally these were very

Mackintosh's of Halifax were one of the first operators to place tilt-cab Mercurys into service in 1965. They carried sugar confectionery in 24' box vans built by Oswald Tillotson Ltd. At the time, the overall specification and performance of the Mercury placed it well ahead of any of its competitors. (AEC)

The well laden Marshal of Thomas Harwood contrasts with the rows of terraced cottages, built in another age of transport. This was chassis No. TGM6RS 353 making its way along an unusually deserted road in Bolton. In the relative terms of history, this evocative photograph dates from only yesterday, but it typifies an era which is long gone. *Thomas Harwood*)

prosperous and profitable years for most hauliers, so many chose to replace old vehicles with new ones, rather than up-date them.

Also in 1968 the existing system of 'A', 'B' and 'C' licences was replaced by an Operators Licence, with the basis for licensing becoming 'quality' rather than 'quantity'. Coupled with this, the inspection of operators' premises, particularly with regard to their suitability and maintenance facilities, became a requirement before 'O' Licences were first issued or renewed.

Apart from having to provide a range of vehicles capable of meeting these legislative requirements, the spin off for AEC was a huge demand for new vehicles, which could not be entirely met by AEC and other home manufacturers, and this was one of the reasons why the importation of European built vehicles started in the mid-1960s.

VEHICLES

The existing medium weight and heavyweight ranges were selling very well and were reliable and popular. However, the cabs were still somewhat noisy and uncomfortable. In 1964 at the autumn Commercial Motor Show. AEC exhibited a range of lorries fitted with a new, all steel construction cab. This was a Leyland group cab and was used on the AEC, Albion and Leyland vehicles. Even though three marques shared this cab, underneath they all retained their own identities and components. The AEC range had several significant changes from the previous models, apart

from the cab. This was the first time that the main AEC goods range had shared the same style of cab. For the export market some bonneted models were retained, and the Militant Mk III still kept a Mk V style cab. It was to be late 1965 before the first AECs with the new style cab entered service, and even well into 1966 some Mammoth Major Mk Vs and Mandator Mk Vs were still being delivered. Some of these vehicles did in fact receive the new AV691 engine.

The new, all steel cab was designed to tilt at an angle of 55° for ease of access to the engine for maintenance purposes. The steering column, driver's seat, and the offside floor pan assembly all remained fixed with the cab tilted. The front end of the chassis was cranked down to enable a low floor height to be utilised with only one entrance step required.

The external dimensions were governed by the requirements of some overseas markets, but the 6' 3" wide and 2' 5" deep windscreen gave an excellent field of vision. The actual styling of the cab was done by Giovanni Michelotti and it was an attractive structure. There was a 7.9 Kw heater which was powerful and efficient. The engine cover was sound and heat insulated, and the roof lining was made from sound absorbing material mounted onto a sheet of consolidated glasswool. The steering wheel was inclined at an angle of 17° to the horizontal and was relatively low in relation to the driver's seat. Mounted around the steering wheel was a binnacle which contained all the instruments and switches. The fuse box and junction box were accessible through a cover in the steering column, and the flasher unit, voltage regulator and warning

Turners Transport of Soham replaced over 10% of their fleet with new tilt-cab AECs in 1966. This 6x2 Marshal carried an insulated, demountable body, designed for hanging meat transport, as well as general produce. It was photographed in 1966 at the long since demolished Ely sugar factory. (*AEC*)

buzzers were located behind the driver's seat, with easy access when the cab was tilted.

The underside of the cab was also covered with sound insulating material. The windscreen wipers were long and swept a large proportion of the windscreen surface area, and they were driven by an air operated motor. This proved to be very troublesome in service and was replaced by an electric motor on many vehicles. The cab structure was mounted on a sub-frame layout for tilting, with the holding down mechanism operated from the nearside. At first there was a lever, lockable with the ignition key to hold the cab in position, but this

was found to be inefficient and could allow the cab to tilt in an emergency braking situation, with known tragic consequences for at least one unfortunate driver. A heavy duty bolt down mechanism replaced this lever.

One man was able to tilt the cab on his own, and it was a big improvement on any previous AEC cab, being comfortable, warm, well ventilated and reasonably quiet for the driver. Many people were tempted to change jobs because they were offered a new AEC to drive. Early cabs were prone to the windscreens falling out, caused by having the doors fully opened with the cab tilted. The aerodynamics were poor, which resulted

in the side windows and mirrors becoming covered with road grime in wet weather. Re-locating the mirror arms to the windscreen pillars helped in this respect.

The cab had been ergonomically designed and they were made by Joseph Sankey Ltd. (later GKN Sankey) of Wellington. Subtle differences in the front grille panel designs helped to distinguish those used for the AEC, Albion, and Leyland lorries, with the first two also having wider front wings which gave the cab a more balanced appearance. These wider wings had also been designed to accommodate 11.00 x 20 wheel and tyre equipment, with which it was intended to fit all the AEC range, but operators, who no doubt were concerned about the extra weight of such wheels and tyres, persuaded AEC to revert to 10.00 x 20 size, and the major tyre manufacturers strengthened their designs in response. Some export models were fitted with 12.00 x 20 tyres. There were three different front grille panel designs used on AECs through the years, but the first, all chromium plated style was the most attractive. Because the engine cover was offset, it was not easy to adapt the cab for left hand control, and this same large engine cover made a satisfactory sleeper cab an impossibility in later years, although when it was first conceived sleeper cabs were very rare in Britain. When mounted on a medium weight chassis the engine installation was neat, but with the larger engine in the heavy weights it was cramped, and a tight installation.

A new engine range was introduced for all the tilt-cabbed vehicles, and they were based on the A470 and A690 engines. These reverted to a dry liner design with re-worked cylinder heads and nitride hardened alloy steel crankshafts. The A470 became the A471/505, and the A690 became the A691/760.

	A471	A505	A691	A760
Bore mm.	112	116	130	136
Stroke mm.	130	130	142	142
Capacity cc	7,685	8,226	11,310	12,473
BHP (std)	130	149	205	226
@ rpm	2,200	2,200	2,200	2,200
Torque Lb.Ft.	368	391	573	618
@ rpm	1,100	1,300	1,200	1,500
Fuel Pump Type	DPA	DPA	DPA	In-Line

The new vehicle range was pre-fixed 'T' to denote 'Tilt Cab'.

Prior to 1970, each AEC model type had its own series of chassis numbers allocated against orders received. The chassis numbers then became sequential irrespective of model type, and they were allocated to vehicles as they were coming down the line at Southall. It is, therefore, not possible to give accurate figures for each type built after 1970.

MERCURY
Type TGM4R
When introduced it was fitted with the AV505 engine, with the AV471 optional. Drive was through a 15⅜" clutch giving a frictional area of 237 sq.ins., and the D197 speed overdrive, constant mesh gearbox. The standard rear axle was a single reduction spiral bevel type with a choice of two ratios. Alternatively, a double

reduction spiral bevel double helical rear axle with a choice of four ratios could be specified. This was standard in the tractor unit. The full air pressure, dual circuit, braking system operated 'S' cam leading and trailing brake shoes. Early Mercurys had Lockheed brake assemblies, but their exposed thread adjusters were prone to seizure, and Girling brake equipment, with covered adjuster threads replaced them on later models. The drums were 15½" diameter and contained 6" wide front, and 8" wide rear brake shoes. The total frictional area was 832 sq.ins. The hand brake was air assisted, and power assisted steering was standard. An exhaust brake was an optional extra. The highest rear axle ratio gave a top speed of 60 mph, and the longest 18' wheelbase version, with a suitable 25' long aluminium alloy flat platform body, gave about 10¼ tons of payload within the 16 tons gross vehicle weight limit.

The Mercury was available with a choice of four wheelbase options, (the shortest one limited the gross vehicle weight to 15 tons), and as a 9' 6" wheelbase tractor unit. This model was initially for 24 tons gross train weight operations, which was later increased to 25 tons, and in 1970, 26 tons. The AV471 engine was not a popular option and was dropped in the late 1960s. In 1968 a rear axle load sensing valve was fitted to the tractor unit, and in 1970 a Leyland Group hub reduction rear axle was fitted in the tractor unit. For the last few months of production the AV505 engine was replaced with the AV 506 engine, which was a de-rated version of its predecessor, with an in-line fuel pump, and re-designed cam shaft, with different injectors.

The last Mercury to be built was a tractor unit, chassis number 5TGM4R 36199, engine number AV506 5AX 551. It was completed on 1st July 1977 and entered service registered WLE 818S with E.J. Masters Ltd., Kings Langley, on 3rd October 1977. Its subsequent history and fate is unknown.

MARSHAL

Type TGM6R
The Marshal was fitted with the AV505 engine and D197 6 speed overdrive constant mesh gearbox, as in the Mercury. The rear axle and bogie options were:—

S suffix: single drive double reduction spiral bevel double helical rear axle with 4 spring compensated underslung suspension, and a choice of four axle ratios.

T suffix: double drive single reduction spiral bevel axles, with a lockable third differential, and 4 spring compensated undersling suspension, with a choice of four axle ratios.

A suffix: double drive axles (as T suffix) with fully articulated 2 spring bogie.

Power assisted steering was standard and the braking system was as for the Mercury, apart from slightly narrower rear brake drums of 7", the total friction area was 1185 sq.ins. The secondary braking system operated on the front and third axles. An exhaust brake was an optional extra. Later Marshals had the

THOMAS HARWOOD

AV505 engine uprated to 165 bhp at 2,400 rpm and a 12 speed constant mesh splitter gearbox was optional. There was a choice of three wheelbase options. In 1971, the gross weight rating was increased by 2 tons to 24 tons, and with the long wheelbase 6 x 2, fitted with a 27' 6" aluminium alloy flat platform body, almost 17 tons of payload became possible.

In 1969 a lightweight eight wheeler, the Marshal Eight, type TGM8R, was introduced at the request of one or two operators and was rated at 24 tons gross vehicle weight. It was not popular, and was deleted from the sales catalogue in 1970. A far more acceptable model, introduced again after operator requests for more power when 24 tons gross vehicle weight operations became permissible on three axles in late 1971, was the Marshal Major, type 2TG6R, and in reality a hybrid Mammoth Major and Marshal.

It was fitted with the AV760 engine and D203 6 speed overdrive constant mesh gearbox. The engine, as installed, was downrated to 180 bhp and fitted with a DPA fuel pump. The heavier engine and gearbox resulted in a loss of payload, but over 15 tons of payload was still possible with the 15' 10" wheelbase tipper versions. The last Marshals to be built were fitted with the AV506 engine.

The last Marshal built was Chassis Number 4TGM6RT 35808, engine number AV506 5BX 522 during May 1977. It was registered DHO 746S and entered service on 7th October 1977 with Simmons Watts Ltd. of Banbury. Its subsequent history and fate is unknown.

MAMMOTH MAJOR

Type TG6R (six wheeler) and
Type TG8R (eight wheeler).
When originally introduced, the Mammoth Majors were fitted with the AV691 engine, with the AV760 engine as the option. The D203 6 speed overdrive constant mesh

For the first 3 years or so of the tilt-cab production, the AEC letters were mounted on the bottom grille panel, and there was no individual model badge. In this position the letters usually fell off, and they were subsequently mounted on the top of the lower panel, with the model name badge being mounted on the lower grille. (*Thomas Harwood*)

gearbox was common to either engine. The AV691 unit had a 16" clutch of 268 sq. ins. frictional area, and a larger 17" clutch of 320 sq. ins. frictional area was fitted to the AV760 engine. The clutch was air assisted, hydraulically operated. The rear axles options were:–

S suffix: single drive double reduction spiral bevel double helical rear axle, with 4 spring compensated underslung suspension, with a choice of four axle ratios.

D suffix: double drive overhead worm reduction axles with a lockable third differential, with 4 spring compensated underslung suspension, and a choice of three axle ratios.

T suffix: double drive double reduction spiral bevel double helical rear axles, with a lockable third differential, and 4 spring compensated underslung suspension, with a choice of 4 axle ratios.

B suffix: double drive axles (as T suffix) with fully articulated 2 spring suspension.

The full air pressure, dual circuit brakes were of the 'S' cam leading and trailing shoe type. There was a separate hand operated emergency parking brake operating on the first and last axles. The 15½" brake drums housed 6" wide front, and 8" wide rear shoes, giving a total frictional area of 1308 sq. ins. on the six wheeler, and 1664 sq. ins. on the eight wheeler. An exhaust brake was an optional extra, and the cam and double roller steering was power assisted. There were two standard wheelbase options for either 22 tons or 24 tons gross vehicle weight operations for the six and eight wheeler respectively, and two wheelbase options available to special order. The longest of these which was 20' 10", allowed the eight wheeler to operate at 26 tons gross weight. The gross train weight for drawbar trailer operations was 32 tons in Britain. The eight wheeler was designed to operate at 28 tons gross vehicle weight and in 1972 was allowed to do so with the longer standard wheel base. By then the AV760 engine had long been the standard unit. The six wheeler gross vehicle weight was also raised to 24 tons. The last 8 wheelers to be built could operate at 30 tons gross vehicle weight, as this limit was raised again in 1975. Where legal restrictions permitted, the gross train weights were 40 tons, and with the 'B' rear bogie option, 56 tons. In 1971 two additional gearbox options became available, a 10 speed constant mesh splitter unit, and a 10 speed constant mesh range change unit.

The Mammoth Major six wheeler was also available as a tractor unit for heavy haulage operations. For a few years up to 1970, some operators also used them as standard 32 tons gross train weight prime movers as a way of overcoming the outer axle spread limitations. They were, however, heavy for normal transport duties, and whilst they were almost indestructible, they suffered a payload penalty of up to two tons when compared with a Mandator or Mammoth Minor in this role. For heavy haulage operations the Mammoth Major tractor unit could be rated at 45 tons, 56 tons, and 65 tons. For these heavier weights a 2 speed auxiliary gearbox was fitted at the rear of, and in unit with the main gearbox. The RAF Mammoth Major six wheeler re-fuellers also had this auxiliary gearbox fitted for drawbar trailer operations at 45 tons gross train weights on airfields.

The last Mammoth Major six wheeler, chassis number 2TG6RB 36379, engine number AV760 5DX 19726 was completed on 19th August 1977. It was delivered to Gloster Saro for equipping as an aircraft refueller, and it is believed to be still in service with the Sultan of Oman's Air Force.

The last Mammoth Major eight wheeler, chassis number 3TG8RT 36433, engine number AV760 5FVX 19731 was completed on 31st August 1977. It was not placed in service until 1979 and it was registered TPO 112T. It was bought for preservation in early 1992 by Kevin Dennis of Wainfleet.

MANDATOR

Type TG4R

The Mandator was originally fitted with the AV691 engine as standard. with the AV760 unit optional, but by 1967 the AV760 was the standard engine. The gearbox was the D203 6 speed overdrive constant mesh unit, with clutch sizes the same as for the Mammoth Major. The clutch was air assisted, hydraulically operated. Final drive was by a double reduction spiral bevel helical rear axle with a choice of four ratios. An extra heavy duty rear axle was an alternative choice. The Mandator was available as a 9' 6" wheelbase tractor unit, or as a 15' or 18' wheelbase rigid for drawbar trailer operations. The tractor unit was rated at 15 tons gross vehicle weight (5 tons front/10 tons rear axle) and 32 tons gross train weight. The long wheelbase Mandator was rated at 16 tons gross vehicle weight. Both had a design gross train weight of 36 tons. The full air pressure, dual circuit brakes were of 'S' cam leading and trailing shoe design, and the 15½" drums housed 6" wide front, and 8" wide rear shoes. The total frictional area was 832 sq.ins. The hand brake was air assisted, and the secondary brakes

were operated by a separate hand control lever. Provisions for 3-line trailer brakes were a part of the system. An exhaust brake was an optional extra, as was power assisted steering. Top speed with the highest rear axle ratio was 62 mph.

In 1968 a 10 speed constant mesh splitter gearbox became an optional choice, as did a semi- automatic gearbox. This was a fluid flywheel with centrifugal lock up clutch, 5 speed direct acting epicyclic gearbox with a unit mounted splitter gear giving 10 forward and two reverse speeds. The semi-automatic gearbox option was de-listed in 1971 to be replaced by the option of a 10 speed constant mesh range change gearbox. In 1968 a load sensing valve was fitted to the rear axle brakes, and an air operated cross axle differential lock was an optional extra. By the end of Mandator production the AV760 engine had been uprated to 265 bhp at 2,200 rpm.

The last Mandator tractor unit, chassis number 2TG4R 36214, engine number AV760 5ETX 19698 was built on 5th July 1977. It was registered YNG 181S and entered service on 1st June 1978 with Alcocks Transport Ltd., Kings Lynn. It is now believed to be in preservation in Scotland.

MAMMOTH MINOR

Type TG6RF

The Mammoth Minor twin steer tractor unit was specifically introduced to allow 32 tons gross train

The 6x4 Marshal was a popular tipper chassis in its 15' 10" wheelbase format, and could provide a 14 ton payload when operating at the 22 tons gross vehicle weight, which applied when this photograph was taken. Based at Dene Quarry, Cromford, Derbys., this Marshal was one of many used by Hoveringham Stone Ltd. (*AEC*)

~120~

The Marshal Eight was introduced as a light weight 24 tons gross vehicle weight eight wheeler, but it did not appeal to many customers, as the AV505 engine was a bit underpowered for heavy duty site work such as this concrete mixer would have to contend with. In an attempt to save even more weight, the one photographed is equipped with tubeless tyres. *(AEC)*

weight operations with reasonable outer axle spreads under the 1964 C. and U. Regulations. The engine, gearbox, and the rear axle options were identical to the Mandator. The vehicle had a gross weight rating of 18 tons, with the front axles rated at 4 tons each. The braking system was identical to the Mandator, and the extra front axle increased the total frictional area to 1188 sq.ins. Power assisted steering was standard and the wheelbase was 12' 2½". Because of the reduction in available chassis space between the second and third axles, the air tanks were mounted on top of the chassis behind the cab, and twin fuel tanks were fitted, one on

each side. The model was dis-continued in 1970, as by then a change in regulations had made it unnecessary.

MANDATOR V8

Type VTG4R

When introduced in 1968 the Mandator V8 took the commercial vehicle industry by storm. It was a high specification, high powered tractor unit, but it was destined to fail miserably. The reasons for its failure are many, but to put it simply, it was a very ambitious vehicle for the time, it was launched prematurely, and it was underdeveloped. The design and development of the

V8-800 engine commenced in 1962 at Southall. It was a 90° configuration dry liner unit of oversquare design. The bore was 130mm and the stroke was 114mm giving a swept volume of 12,154 litres. It was rated at 247 bhp at 2,600 rpm. The torque figure of 580 lb. ft. at 1,400 rpm was surprisingly low, and indicated that to obtain the best performance from this engine it would be necessary to keep the revs high. From the outset it was designed for eventual turbo-charging and inter-cooling, with a potential output of up to 400 bhp to provide AEC and the Leyland Group with a high power engine for the 1970s and 1980s.

To accommodate this engine a wider Mandator chassis was necessary, and a new version of the tilt cab, called the 'Thru-Way' cab was made. Visually this cab was externally identical to the existing cab, but as the name implied it had been re-designed internally to a walk through type. Because the V8-800 engine was shorter than the in-line AV760 unit, it was set back in the chassis, and this enabled the large engine cover of the standard cab to be removed. The standard gearbox was a 10 speed Pneumocyclic semi-automatic unit, which consisted of a fluid clutch and an air operated 5 speed epicyclic gearbox with a front mounted overdrive

splitter unit. Alternative gearboxes were the D203 6 speed overdrive constant mesh unit, or the 10 speed constant mesh splitter gearbox. A 17" clutch with 320 sq.ins. frictional area was fitted for these optional manual gearboxes, and it was operated hydraulically with air assistance. Final drive was through the normal Mandator double reduction spiral bevel double helical rear axle, with a choice of three ratios. A slightly increased front axle rating of 5.4 tons was used. The brake drum and shoe dimensions were identical to the TG4R model, but the main service brake system incorporated a load sensing valve, and the parking brake was a power assisted lock actuator type operating on all four wheels. Power assisted steering was optional, and the top speed with the highest rear axle ratio was 66 mph.

Engine trials were conducted in such diverse climates as Finland, France, Australia, South Africa, and Austria and in 1967 the first home operator trials commenced with selected fleets. Western Transport, Russell of Bathgate, and Turners (Soham) Ltd., were amongst the few operators chosen. Turners received chassis number VTG4R 005, registered NGJ 294D, and even today several drivers who were allocated to it can

Livestock hauliers Cooks of Reading, placed in service this high specification horse box in 1969. The insulated, air conditioned body was built by Lambourne Engineering on a Marshal chassis, and it was mainly used on continental journeys. (*AEC*)

recall the startling performance of the vehicle. Well
remembered is a race along the A1 one night from
Grantham to Alconbury Hill with the Russell Mandator
V8. They both overtook everything else on the road,
including cars!

Some 350 Mandator V8s entered service in
Britain, but they soon started to give problems. They
were prone to overheating and this could result in the
pistons picking up on the liners. A later, 135mm wide
bore engine of 13.1 litres and thinner cylinder liners did
not suffer to the same extent with this particular fault.
The big end crankshaft journals were rather narrow and
this caused problems. The semi-automatic gearbox gave
trouble, and some operators claimed that the splitter
switch was very sensitive and could cause high engine
revs. unexpectedly, so resulting in engine damage.
Eventually the model was withdrawn and AEC
proceeded to buy most of them back. A handful of
Mammoth Major V8 powered six wheeled tractor units
had also been built.

Some Mandator V8s soldiered on, and operators
who were prepared to change the big end shells every
50-60,000 miles got several years service out of them
with sensible drivers. Boon Bros. of Whittlesey operated
Mandator V8 NJE 514H for 7 years before withdrawing
it in February 1976. At least eight Mandator V8s are
known to have survived in running order: significantly
all of them have D203 constant mesh gearboxes fitted. It
has been written that the disaster with the Mandator V8
was ultimately responsible for the demise of AEC, but
that is nonsense. Whilst it was certainly a severe blow to
AEC, and their first ever total failure, they still enjoyed a
lot of customer loyalty and goodwill and such an
ambitious project was seen for what it was – a vehicle

before its time – which if developed further before being
launched could have succeeded. Air Products Ltd.
placed several Mandator V8s into service and
experienced many of the problems, but they continued
to buy AECs for as long as they were made.

LEYLAND MARATHON
Type 2T25/27

The Leyland Marathon was designed to be a high
specification, premium tractor unit and load carrier, to
combat the growing imports of such types. After the
demise of the V8-800 engine, the AEC A760 was the
only unit in the Leyland Group capable of being
developed further to provide the power and reliability
required for such a vehicle. Consequently the AV760
was re-designed and turbo-charged to become the TL12
engine. The Marathon concept also allowed for the
fitting of proprietary engines from Cummins and Rolls
Royce if customers wished to specify them. Whilst the
Marathon could not be regarded as a 'true AEC' in the
sense that it was not developed from a preceding AEC
model, it was developed and built at Southall from 1973
until 1979, and as such should be recognised.

The TL12 engine was rated at 280 bhp at 2,200
rpm, with a torque output of 780 lb.ft. at 1,300 rpm. It
retained the cylinder dimensions of the A760 unit, which
being adopted for the turbo-charging had re-designed
cylinder heads and other detail changes. The gearbox
was the Fuller Roadranger 9 speed range change
constant mesh unit, and final drive was via a Leyland
Group hub reduction rear axle. The suspension featured
a new taper leaf design. The cab was a raised version of
the existing Sankey tilt cab and was available with a
factory fitted sleeper cab option. Mechanically, the

RHM Agriculture had a very large fleet of Marshals, and this neatly sheeted load belies the fact that this is a tipper. The bodies were designed to be used in either mode; as a tipper for bulk grain and animal feed, or as a flat for palletised loads with the sides folded down. Dalgety bought the RHM businesses, and the last remaining Marshals were withdrawn in 1986.
(*Motorphoto*)

Marathon was reliable from its introduction, but it was let down by its detail finish, sure signs of a vehicle being developed in a rush within severe budget constraints. Control cables and linkages, air piping runs, and door catches all caused problems. The suspension damper settings were ill-matched and the ride was harsh as a result.

The Marathon performed well, but drivers were not particularly happy with them. When the Mk II version was introduced in 1977, most of the detail faults had been eradicated and the cab was re-trimmed to improve the interior. This version was well received, popular, and it sold well.

Many former Mandator operators bought the Marathon because it was produced at Southall, and they often fitted the AEC letters to the lower grille. There is firm evidence to suggest that it was intended to badge the Marathon as an AEC on its launch, but this decision was changed and they were badged entirely as Leylands. The TL12 engine proved to be an excellent unit in service, reliable and capable of high mileages before overhaul. When Southall was closed, the production of the TL12 engine was transferred to Leyland, and this unit was used in the new T45 Leyland Roadtrain range introduced in 1981, By 1983 it had been dropped from the range, simply because the economics of producing relatively small numbers of engines dictated that it was more beneficial to purchase proprietary units. The last Marathon to be built at Southall, chassis number 2T25/101 38920 was completed on 4th April 1979.

SUMMARY
OF THE TILT-CAB RANGE

The launch of the tilt-cab range saw the best features of the preceding medium weight, and heavy weight Mk V ranges, combined with detail changes to the major components, and the new cab common to the AEC marque. For several years after their introduction they were very successful and popular models. By the time production had ceased they had become somewhat dated when compared to some of the imported makes, although they were still reliable, and cost effective to operate in many applications.

When introduced, they were equipped with Butec alternators and starter motors. Butec had been formed as a Leyland Group subsidiary to manufacture these components in an attempt to combat the near monopoly enjoyed by CAV, who had absorbed Simms Motor Units. The designs Butec used were from the Leece Neville Company of Ohio, and from the outset the alternators were not capable of sustained high load outputs. Many of them had to be replaced under warranty until improvements in the design were made. The starter motors were reliable but could retain water thrown up by the tyres in wet conditions. They had been designed for use with a totally enclosed flywheel, as used in the USA, and not for an open flywheel as commonly used on British vehicles. In time, corrosion occurred, resulting in a starter motor short circuit. There were many recorded incidents of AECs mysteriously starting themselves up. Again, modifications to the design were required.

Early models suffered from the radiator plastic header tanks bursting, and the plastic fan blades could be thrown forward into the radiator, causing serious damage. Problems with overheating, particularly with the AV691 engine, were as a result of poor cooling from the low, partially obstructed radiator, and lack of water-head in the too small, plastic, header tank. These tanks were eventually replaced on all models with a larger, mild steel tank mounted behind the cab. The design of the cab dictated that air circulation around the AV691/760 engine installation was restricted, as was the radiator capacity. All tilt-cab models would probably have benefited from a larger capacity radiator.

The Sankey cabs were rather prone to rusting

R. Sinclair Ltd. of Evesham were AEC operators for many years, and this 1974 Mercury had the optional heavy duty bumper bar fitted, with a central towing pin. (*C.V.R.T.C.*)

toughness, ruggedness, durability, and reliability of their illustrious predecessors, and they were a popular multi-axle heavy weight range. The Mandator was an excellent prime-mover when introduced and with the AV760 engine the performance was unmatched by any comparable British produced tractor unit for several years. It was eventually surpassed by the high specification, premium imported makes, and even then it continued to be an excellent fleet tractor unit. In 1970, a new Mandator could be put into service for approximately £4,400 and that represented great value for money, with earnings and economics that were hard to beat.

POLICY

By the mid 1960s some very fundamental changes in AEC's business were coming into effect. They had always been regarded as primarily a passenger chassis builder who also built goods vehicles, but this emphasis was changing rapidly. Allied to this was the growing dominance of a Group senior management with a bias towards the Leyland philosophy. Sales of conventional buses, traditionally a strong AEC market, had been in serious decline for some years, and the front entrance, rear engine double deck models introduced by AEC's competitors in the late 1950s had started to badly undermine their chassis sales. AEC had built one such rear engine prototype bus using mainly Routemaster components, and this had entered service with London Transport, but no more had been built. The last Routemaster was delivered to London Transport in 1968, and in the same year the last Regent V was also delivered.

For the first time in 50 years AEC had no double deck bus business, and in the sales catalogue were just the Reliance coach, the rear engine Swift/Merlin single deck bus, and the Ranger bus, which was a simple and rugged design for the Third World countries, and which was based on the Mercury chassis. The very high level of sales achieved with the introduction of the tilt-cab goods range more than offset the loss of the bus business for a few years. For example, Turners of Soham placed a total of 35 Mercurys and Mandators in service in 1966, out of a fleet total of some 220 lorries. BRS were still buying in quantity and they were allowed to call off chassis from Southall as they required them without placing advance orders. The specialist vehicles such as the Dumptruk were still popular, with 100 such machines going into service with just five contractors alone in 1967.

throughout the life of the range, although the early cabs were probably not quite as bad as the later ones. Certainly, severe cab corrosion caused the premature withdrawal of many mechanically sound AECs.

The thickness of the cylinder liners in the AV691 engines could lead to heat retention in the cylinders, but the thinner cylinder liners used in the AV760 engine allowed quicker heat dissipation, and were much better. Later AV505 engines could be prone to pistons picking up on cylinder liners, due entirely to a lack of money being made available for the AV505 engine manufacturing machinery at Southall. Installed for the AV470 engine, this machinery had become worn, and inaccurate machining of the cylinder block could take place. This resulted in a minute air pocket occurring when the cylinder liners were pressed in and this could be sufficient to cause a localised hot spot on the liner. Generally speaking, the AV505 engine was an excellent and reliable unit throughout most of its production life, and was capable of high mileages between overhauls. Similarly the AV760 engine was a robust and efficient unit.

For many years the Mercury TGM4R was an outstanding four wheeler and it was a formidable revenue earner with modest running costs. Long wheelbase versions could suffer from propeller shaft centre bearings trouble, but this fault was eventually cured. The Mercury tractor unit was a very useful lorry, and gave up to 18½ tons of payload when operating at 26 tons gross train weight. Similarly, the Marshal TGM6R was an excellent machine in all respects. The 6 x 4 versions could experience third differential problems because they were weak, and the AV505 engine was perhaps a little underpowered for some 24 tons gross vehicle weight applications. The vast majority of the medium weight range vehicles gave operators years of trouble free and profitable service.

The Mammoth Majors continued the traditions of

Things were not going as well on the overseas front. The hitherto successful AEC/Willeme association in France was terminated in favour of a Leyland/Hotchkiss deal, but this fell through leaving the Leyland Group without any representation there. An identical situation occurred in Holland, and in South America the Siam di Tella agreement was terminated in favour of another which failed to materialise. The failure

T.J.E. Price Ltd. of Cardiff were Thornycroft operators who changed to AECs after the ACV takeover of the Basingstoke company in 1961. They continued to run AECs until the mid-1980s, and this 1975 Mercury features the final style of front grille. Also, by this time, the chrome bumper bar was no longer fitted as standard. (*Motorphoto*)

of this latter deal, which had been for local CKD chassis assembly, resulted in AEC losing a presence in Argentina, because shortly afterwards the importation of completed chassis was stopped. There were a few other similar instances world wide, and AEC's exports, traditionally always a strong and prosperous sector for them, were distinctly on the wane, yet none of this was directly attributable to AEC or its vehicles, but to wrong Group management decisions.

In 1968 the merger of the Leyland Group and BMC, which included Jaguar, Daimler, and Guy was announced. This brought about more model duplication, and serious financial, and labour relations problems with the volume car making division. Within a very short period of time, the profits made by the heavy goods vehicle divisions had to be directed to the loss making car division to keep the business viable. Consequently, capital which should have been used to improve the goods vehicle ranges was not available. In particular, development of the quality heavy models was essential to ward off growing imports of high specification tractor units from European manufacturers. The engineering excellence of these imported makes was certainly no better than AEC's, but their turbo-charged engines and multi-ratio transmissions, together with a well appointed and comfortable cab, made such trucks ideally suited to Motorway running both at home and in Europe. Whilst the Mandator was reliable and popular and still selling well, it could not compete with the high specification Volvo F88, or Scania 140, on overall performance and driver appeal. The concept for such a vehicle was born with the Marathon, and given the limited time scale, and small development budget provided for it, it did reasonably well.

For some time AEC managers had been very

reluctantly bowing to Leyland influence, as the old Leyland management appeared to come to the forefront of affairs. From the early days of the merger there had been clashes of personality at the top level. Too many people had old scores to settle and they used every opportunity they could to do so, often to the detriment of the business. AEC often felt that they were the guinea pigs for new ideas, such as the semi-automatic gearbox used in the Mandator V8, and the Butec components used for the tilt-cab range. In 1970 the Famous Blue Triangle was removed from the AEC grille panel along with the AEC hub logos. They were replaced with a Leyland Group badge, but the AEC lower grille letters were retained. Many operators continued to remove the Leyland badges, and replace them with the correct AEC logos when they took delivery of their new vehicle.

A valuable insight into the way in which decisions were being made has been gained by the detailed examination of a lengthy document prepared in early 1971, which discusses the options available for the AEC lorry range. Then, AEC was producing at some 77% of its total annual chassis capacity, and because the similar sized production plant at Leyland was at full capacity, it was recommended that AEC should develop and produce the FPT 70 premium goods range, (Marathon), for launching in late 1973.

Also recommended was the re-launch of the Mandator V8 in September 1971, and the fitting of the higher (5½") datum cab (as used on the Leyland Lynx etc.) to the AEC range to provide better cooling and reliability. Only the Marathon recommendation was accepted. From this document it is obvious that everything that could be done to further the Leyland built range would be done. In 1970 AEC had built almost 3,000 medium-weights of the Mercury and

The Marshal Major
was fitted with a
down-rated AV760
engine to provide
more power and
torque than the
standard AV505
unit. John
Jempson & Son
Ltd. of Rye were
AEC operators for
many years, and
were one of the
last large fleets to
continue using
them, until well
into the 1980s.
(*Motorphoto*)

Marshal type, and they were outselling the corresponding Leyland Lynx and Bison models by a ratio of 3½:1. In addition to this, Guy had built over 1,000 medium-weights in 1970 powered by the AV505 engine.

At the time the AEC Mercury was without question the finest four wheeler on the road, and whilst its competitor the Lynx was a fairly new model, there is tacit admittance in this document that the Lynx and Bison would never gain a satisfactory market share whilst the Mercury and Marshal were still in production, because of the customer loyalty AEC enjoyed. Obviously here was a classic case of model duplication, yet it was proposed that the successful AECs be phased out so that the unpopular models, which were also experiencing serious problems with the Leyland 500 series engine, could prosper. There was no suggestion of developing the Mercury and Marshal further to capitalise on the good reputation and loyalty they enjoyed with operators. As it happened the Mercury and Marshal did continue for a few more years, but no serious development took place, and their Leyland rivals never achieved what was expected of them.

During the early 1970s the serious financial problems of the British Leyland Motor Corporation (BLMC), as the former Leyland Group had then become, were reaching crisis proportions. The heavy vehicles division was still profitable, but overall this massive organisation was showing a huge loss. Coupled to this were extensive and high borrowings, resulting in no investment in either new vehicles, replacement manufacturing machinery, or the upgrading of buildings, necessary to comply with new Health and Safety at Work legislation being introduced at the time.

By 1974 BLMC was effectively bankrupt, but there were tremendous pressures being exerted from within the Group, and from the Government and Trade Unions for BLMC to be preserved in its entirety, rather than for it to be disbanded and the profitable parts split from the loss makers. This all led to direct Government intervention and the state funded National Enterprise Board moved in to acquire 95% of the shares, with the formation of British Leyland Ltd. This resulted in a complete reorganisation, and at long last each division within the company was made financially autonomous and independent. However, it was a case of too little too late and the severe investment starvation of the preceding years had taken its toll.

Confidence had been lost by employees and customers alike, and there was a severe loss of orders in all sectors of the business. By now as these events were unfolding AEC was becoming a victim of the new policies and as production levels dwindled at Southall it was apparent that closure was not too far ahead.

The Southall site had seen very little expansion since the early 1960s, and the large expanse of sports fields there had always been sacrosanct, with the erection of buildings upon them being prohibited. In the early 1970s there was, by the standards of 1993, full employment, and the recruitment of skilled labour was very difficult. As production levels dwindled, then staffing levels also fell. The Swift/Merlin bus ceased production in 1972, with no replacement model, and from the mid 1970s the production of 'true' AEC lorries steadily fell. The lack of money for machinery repairs and replacements took its toll on quality. Some customers were stubbornly loyal as it became increasingly difficult for them to obtain an AEC.

A final triumph for operator pressure was the introduction of the L12 engine into the Leyland Buffalo

tractor unit and Bison six wheeler. This engine was a normally aspirated version of the TL12, but it did not breathe very well and was only an adequate performer. Some of the oil and petroleum distributing companies still insisted on the Mandator, and so ensured that it continued in production. It was still a good medium distance fleet distribution tractor unit. Some eight wheeler buyers, particularly those involved with sand and gravel contracting, hearing of the imminent demise of the AEC range, bought Mammoth Majors and stored them for later use. At least one such operator placed four lorries in storage.

The last 'true' AECs were built in the middle and final months of 1977, and by then the Dumptruk production had long been transferred to Aveling Barford. Appropriately enough the last AEC to be built

was a Mammoth Major Eight: after all AEC had built the first one in 1934. All that was left to produce was the Marathon, Reliance, and the Ranger, and it was obvious that Southall no longer had any place in the future plans of British Leyland Ltd. In the final months of Southall, former employees, visitors, and other writers have all commented that an air of sadness and despondency was apparent. The run-down and decay was obvious for all to see.

For almost all of its existence it had been a busy and vibrant place, even exciting when at full capacity, producing 40 or so chassis each day. Arrangements were made to transfer the Marathon production to Scammell at Watford, and the TL12 engine production to Leyland.

On the 25th May 1979, the AEC factory at Southall closed with the loss of 2,150 jobs.

Even into the 1980 the economics c using the mediur weight AECs for loca work were hard t beat, and it was on terminal ca corrosion whicl caused many to be withdrawn. Thi Boston based Marsha was photographe delivering a load c sugar beet to th Spalding factory o the British Suga Corporation (*Bill Taylor*

EPILOGUE

AEC owners remained loyal into the 1980s, continuing to operate lorries well past their normal replacement time. Spiers of Melksham, and John Jempson Ltd. of Rye were but two such hauliers whose Mandators were a familiar sight on the roads during those years. British Leyland Ltd. frequently raised the price of AEC spare parts, and this was seen by some people as a deliberate attempt to force AECs from the road. Some large AEC operators even had their credit terms stopped with the dealers. Maybe British Leyland thought that if AECs were forced out of service, then they could be replaced by Leylands, but they were more often than not replaced by other makes, usually of European origin.

Now in the 1990s it is very rare to see an AEC lorry in revenue earning service in Britain. A few Mercurys and Marshals still earn their keep, and some faithful Mandators are retained as battered yard shunters: they can be guaranteed to start at the first touch of the button on the coldest of mornings. Matadors haul trees in the forests and perform specialist winching tasks elsewhere. Several heavy recovery experts use Mammoth Majors or Militants, and the RAF is dependent upon its Mammoth Major re-fuellers and de-icers. A journey to Malta or Cyprus is guaranteed to be rewarded with the sights and sounds of many AECs in arduous service.

So what can be concluded about AEC, its vehicles, and achievements over the years? This history has attempted not to be an eulogy for the marque, but to be an objective and accurate account of the company, its policies, and the lorries produced, together with some of the weaknesses and faults through the years, which were more than balanced by the many good points they had. The perfect goods vehicle has yet to be produced, but there cannot be any doubt that AEC lorries were one of the leading makes ever to be manufactured in this country. In their heyday they could, and did, compete with any other make both at home and overseas.

Plenty of transport firms were founded with AECs, and flourished and prospered with them. Many a driver, this author included, always felt they were driving a lorry which was a little bit special and perhaps superior to any other lorry on the road.

The 1962 merger with Leyland sealed the eventual fate of AEC. At that time they were the two leading British heavy goods vehicles manufacturers, serving identical markets with a similar range at home and abroad. Reminiscences from those years, and research for this book have highlighted how two, outwardly similar concerns, were so diverse in terms of management policy, philosophy and style. They had totally different attitudes to customers and after-sales service. In deference to former senior executives from both companies who are still alive, some factual evidence concerning the AEC and Leyland rivalry has been withheld, but the full story will be told one day. Suffice it to say that such a merger was never going to work with a Chief Executive appointed from either company, whoever it might have been. Once the politicians started to interfere, and the mass produced car makers were thrown into the melting pot, then the final outcome was inevitable. If AEC had to go then it was better that it went entirely, rather than have 'badge engineered' models of inferior status perpetuate the name. After all, an AEC was a thoroughbred.

In making this statement the author is acutely aware that many employees dedicated their working lives to AEC, and the loss of their company, and their jobs, was a painful blow, but they can be immensely proud of the vehicles they produced.

Whilst selecting the photographs for this book

from many hundreds of AEC shots, and from personal memories of the lorries in service, a common thread for the operation of AECs was sought. In truth it was difficult to find such a thread because ownership ranged from the largest own account and haulage fleets, to the small family business and owner driver. However, maybe one clue does emerge. Today, the 'just in time delivery' concept is the vogue, but there have always been certain types of transport where reliability and promptness were of paramount importance, particularly before the widespread usage of refrigerated transport. The carriage of milk and fresh produce has always been sensitive and for the bulk haulage of milk from the Welsh Borders or the South West, to the bottling dairies of the Midlands and London, it was usually an AEC tanker that was used. Similarly, from the fenlands of East Anglia and Lincolnshire, and Kent's lush Garden of England, then scores of lorries made their way nightly to the wholesale markets of the towns and cities. Invariably it would be an AEC which was entrusted to get the produce there on time. All of these milkmen, growers, and produce carriers needed and depended upon reliable lorries. They chose to purchase AECs.

PRESERVATION

In recent years the preservation of larger goods vehicles has become more common, and a good cross-section of

AEC lorries made through the years has been restored and preserved. The AEC Society was founded in 1983 by Brian Goulding and it has grown to become a thriving and successful appreciation group for the AEC marque. The President of the AEC Society, Harry Pick, has a lifetimes experience of AECs, and as an experienced and highly skilled engineer, his advice has been invaluable to many AEC restorers. The spares situation for most of the later models is still quite good, with some former AEC operators still retaining caches of parts. When a display of AECs is mounted at events such as Truckfest, and many other shows, there is always a tremendous amount of interest shown in the lorries.

Whenever true lorry men meet, the talk usually comes round to AEC, and seldom is a bad word heard about them, as there is still an enormous amount of goodwill towards them. They are held in respect for the high quality of their build, and for the exacting standards of engineering and innovation carried down through the years. There now does appear to be a certain charisma about an AEC, and this is confirmed by the thousands of enthusiasts who make their way to Wollaton Park, Nottingham, on the Spring Bank Holiday weekend every year to attend the AEC Rally. This interest, and the efforts of the dedicated AEC restorers and preservationists will ensure that AEC lorries and the achievements of the people who designed and built them, will never be forgotten.

The London Brick Company has several landfill schemes for disused claypits, and this Marshal was operated as a waste skip carrier. It was one of the last batch of Marshals supplied to LBC in 1976-77, and these remained in service until 1985. (*Motorphoto*)

Top right: For many years, whilst in the service of A.L. Lomas & Sons, of Laughton, this 1976 AV506 engined Marshal was a familiar sight on the A1, hauling potatoes from East Anglia to South Yorkshire. It was still in service when this photograph was taken on 3rd November 1988, and it was finally withdrawn in 1991. (*Author*)

Middle left: When photographed on 22nd June 1989, this Mercury tanker had completed 20 years in service. Withdrawn by Spur Petroleum Ltd. of Bury later that year, it was sold for further service with an asphalt laying contractor. It carried a 2,000 gallon tank on a 12' 1" wheelbase chassis. (*Author*)

Bottom right: Perhaps Mammoth Marshal would be an apt description for Frank Smith's AEC. It started life as a 6x4 Marshal Major in 1974, but in the late 1980s the rear bogie from a 6x2 Mammoth Major was substituted. Seen here waiting to tip at Spiller's Cambridge mill on 29th March 1990, it was still in service in 1993. (*Author*)

Top right: This smart Irish registered Marshal was caught on film in September 1990, on the outskirts of Cambridge, where it had probably been attending the large tractor auctions, frequently held at Milton. (*Craig Temple*)

Top right: Rod Brown of Sutton Bridge uses this 1973 Mercury every day, transferring peas and beans from storage to a canning factory at Long Sutton. Its original owners were D. & E. Salter who used it on produce deliveries. (*Author*)

Middle right: Another long service Mercury, operated by John Hargreaves Ltd. of Stalybridge. It had completed almost 17 years of work, when seen in Huddersfield on 16th January 1990. The driver said that the engine was "still a cracker, and I would take this lorry anywhere". (*Author*)

Bottom left: Still in service in 1992 at 23 years old was this 1969 Mercury, operated by Keith Smith of Stickney, Lincs. When this photograph was taken on 14th July 1990, it had just completed the hectic pea harvest schedules, which often requires day and night working to get the peas to the freezer processing plants. (*Bill Taylor*)

Middle left: Whatever the load is on the Starr Roadways Mammoth Major Six tractor unit, it is certainly very heavy, judging by the way the low-loader is bending, and the tyre spread on the AEC rear bogie. The Mammoth Major dates from 1967. (*Starr Roadways*)

Bottom right: The Boston area of Lincolnshire was awash with AECs, with hauliers large and small using them. This shot of Boston Cattle Market, taken on 14th November 1970 features GJL 666E, a 1967 Mandator of H. Baxter & Son Ltd. with a 40' semi-trailer loaded with tree trunks, and in the background is an AEC of Benton Bros. (*Bill Taylor*)

Top right: The Mammoth Minor tractor unit was popular with the oil and petroleum distributors because they could take advantage of the maximum pay load offered by the 32 tons gross train weight legislation, within a comfortable overall vehicle length. (*Arthur Ingram*)

Top right: Leaving Chancelot Mill, Leith are two Mammoth Minors, each coupled to tandem axle semi-trailers. The side shot of the first one perfectly illustrates the positioning of the air tanks behind the cab. Owned by Allied Mills Ltd., this mill supplies breadmaking flour to much of Scotland, and to the Sunblest Bakery at Gateshead. At the time this photograph was taken, that bakery was the largest bread producer in Europe, using over 400 tons of flour weekly, causing the AECs to be double shifted to keep it supplied. (*AEC*)

Middle right: The lorry driver of the year competition was always well supported by the oil distribution companies, and the Continental Oil Mammoth Minor driver tackles the reversing test. (*Motorphoto*)

Bottom right: Air Products operated this Mammoth Major Six tractor unit at 32 tons gross train weight. The pressurised tanks were built to exacting standards to withstand the limits imposed upon them, and were heavy as a consequence. (*Arthur Ingram*)

Bottom right: A scene repeated hundreds of times every day as a driver asks for directions. A very much travel stained Mammoth Major Six heavy haulage tractor. One of the drawbacks of the tilt-cab is just discernable; the driver's overnight case is in the windscreen because of the distinct lack of stowage within. (*Starr Roadways*)

Left: Lye Trading Company Ltd. operated many AECs for several years, and this Saturday morning photograph of nine of their Mandators shows them loaded with steel, washed down, and ready for the following Monday. (*AEC*)

Left: On the A16 at Scampton on 17th February 1971, this Mandator and tri-axle tipping semi-trailer. Substitute 'super single' tyres onto the trailer and it could well be in use today, at the 38 tonnes gross train weight limit, instead of the then 32 tons limit. (*Bill Taylor*)

Right: The Bradford based Leathers Chemicals were committed AEC users, and this 1969 Mandator is coupled to a tri-axle acid tanker semi-trailer. The trailer does appear to be over-length for the time; an impression gained by the author when he first saw them on the road. *(Arthur Ingram)*

Left & below: The installation of the V8 engine allowed a total re-design of the Mandator tilt-cab, and these photographs illustrate what a difference the removal of the intrusive in-line engine cover made. *(AEC)*

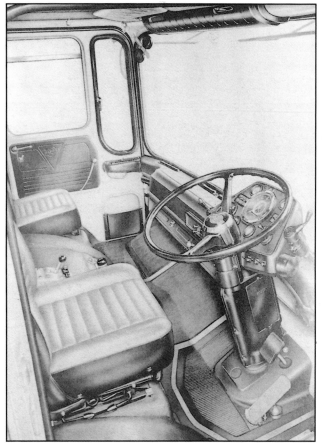

Top right: On display at the 1968 Kent County Show, Percy Henley's new Mandator V8. It is coupled to a new, maximum length semi-trailer carrying an ISO standard length, 39' container. V8s normally carried the larger 'Mandator' badge in the centre of the upper grille. As they had a lower radiator than the AV760 engined Mandator, a special guard has been fabricated for this one. (*Jack Henley*)

Middle left: Considering that relatively few Mandator V8s were produced, and for the majority of them their service life was short, a high proportion of them were photographed in service. Captured for posterity at Monsanto Chemicals, Newport, South Wales, this memorable shot not only portrays the AEC, but also the lorry driver's job. So much of what is happening on the trailer would not be permitted today, yet only a few years ago it was common practice, and anyone who has ever worked on general haulage will readily identify themselves with this scene. (*AEC*)

Bottom left: This is a gem of a photograph taken on the M1 By Arthur Ingram. It highlights several contrasts, apart from the obvious one of the tank contents. The tilt-cab Mandator is, in fact, a V8 model, which could hardly be termed successful, and the Mammoth Major Eight Mk V was arguably one of Southall's best ever models. The V8 cab was capable of carrying its driver and two passengers in comfort, and three men are squeezed into the Mk V's cab. (*Arthur Ingram*)

Top left: Less than 10 Mammoth Major Six V8 tractor units entered service, and the one photographed here is something of a prototype. It has received a higher version of the thru-way cab, and is fitted with Leyland Group hub reduction rear axles. It was powered by the V8-801 engine of 13.1 litres capacity, rated at 272 bhp at 2,600 rpm and 638 lb.ft. of torque at 1,400 rpm. It was designed to operate at 44 tons gross train weight. It is interesting to note how the AEC engineers and designers had adapted the higher datum cab by retaining the standard AEC front panels, and covering the deficit with a deeper bumper bar. As the fitting of this higher cab to all the AEC range was considered, then if AEC versions had been produced using this frontal style, they would have looked far less of a 'bodge-up' than the corresponding Leyland models did. *(AEC)*

Middle right: Possibly only a few months old when photographed on 14th October 1970, a smart Mandator belonging to Fred Sherwood of Long Whatton, Loughborough. It has a good load of timber on a Ferrymasters demountable flat, and the AEC is running on tubeless tyres. *(Bill Taylor)*

Bottom right: For 10 years or so, until the mid 1970s, the tilt-cab Mandator was the mainstay of many general haulage fleets, and this 1970 version is typical of that particular role. It was owned by Fosters Transport of Langworth, Lincoln. *(Motorphoto)*

Top right: Short wheel base Mammoth Major Eight tippers were quite common, although their payload was relatively small when operating at 24 tons gross vehicle weight. This one has a later style of front grille panel, no doubt because of corrosion problems with its original one. (*Author's collection*)

Middle left: Well laden with gravel, this 1972 Mammoth Major Eight comes up the incline out of the quarry in the Mendip Hills, Somerset. It is fitted with super single rear wheels and tyres, not a common option at any time on Mammoth Majors. (*AEC*)

Below: Laden with 'brown reels' of paper, the Mandator of Maurice Hill, Pleasley, Mansfield, overtakes a Mammoth Major Eight Mk V of the London Brick Company, on the M1 in Bedfordshire. (*Arthur Ingram*)

Top right: The last series of Mammoth Major Eights to be designed could operate at up to 30 tons gross vehicle weight, as outer axle spreads were reduced in later years to more workable limits. This one has received a short chassis extension, for bodying with a flat platform. *(AEC)*

Middle right: Fully loaded with bricks, and equipped with a centre mounted Hiab crane, this Ibstock Mammoth Major Eight leans impressively as it negotiates a roundabout. This 1976 model operated at 30 tons gross vehicle weight, and represented the final development of the lorry which could trace its ancestry back to 1934. *(Motorphoto)*

Bottom right: This 1976 Mandator was over 5 years old when photographed in the early 1980s, and the nearside door is showing signs of serious corrosion. The last months of Mandator production included several rigids, most of them being built to special order. *(Motorphoto)*

Right: One of the last Mandators to leave Southall, and by then many AECs had received sleeper cabs. Because of the large engine cover, access to and from the bunk was not easy, and at best, these were only makeshift additions to the standard cab. (*Motorphoto*)

Below: At the peak of their operations, Machins of Spalding were one of the big AEC fleets, and they remained loyal users to the end of production. This 1975 Mandator was photographed on local work in the 1980s delivering sugar beet to the Spalding processing factory. After several years of decline this famous haulier went into receivership in 1992, and the business folded. (*Bill Taylor*)

Top right: A somewhat battered Mammoth Major Eight waits to unload at a sawmill. It has received a sleeper cab conversion, and it has a rear mounted crane. The chassis is filled up with hydraulic oil tank and tackle box, leaving no spare room at all. (*Ken Durston*)

Middle right: Heatons of St. Helens ran Mandator and drawbar trailer combinations, and photographed here is a 1976 example. The payload of such an outfit was about 21 tons, but more often than not it was load volume which was important in deciding to operate these vehicles. (*Ken Durston*)

Below: Many Mandators ended their days as shunters, where the low cab height made them a favourite with drivers who had to climb in and out dozens of times a day. This one ended up at Boston Docks for several years, and it is interesting to compare its registration number with the John Hargreaves Mercury. (*Bill Taylor*)

TUPLIN & SON

LEYLAND

2

CTL 660T

Like many AEC operators, Tuplins of Friskney bought the Marathon because of the Southall production factor. This Mk.II was only 3 weeks old when it was photographed on the 24th August 1978. (*Bill Taylor*)

Left: Spiers of Melksham equipped most of their Mandators with sleeper cab conversions, and many of the last ones they bought came from the oil company fleets. These remained in service until the late 1980s, and fleet number 33, a 1977 model, was photographed in the 1980s with a load of carbon black in tote bins, destined for the Avon Rubber Company Ltd. (*Ken Durston*)

Top right: These two long wheelbase Mandator re-fuellers served at Jersey Airport from 1977 until 1990-91, when they returned to Britain for further airfield duties. When fully laden with jet engine fuel, they each gross 19 tons, and are fitted with 12.00x20 tyres. When photographed in August 1989, their crews still preferred them to any other make of vehicle on the strength, because of the low cab height, and they were "100% reliable". (*Author*)

Middle left: Believed to still be in service in 1993, after being re-cabbed for the second time in its life, Nelstrop's Mammoth Major Eight flour tanker had just discharged its load at the Harvestime Bakery, Walsall, on a dull 5th July 1990, when this photograph was taken. (*Author*)

Below left: Built in 1969 as a 65 tons gross train weight heavy haulage tractor for Wynns of Newport, Ratcliffes still extensively use this 6x4 Mammoth Major. It has had a chassis extension, and is equipped with Holmes 750 recovery gear; it has also been re-cabbed. (*Author*)

Below: En-route for the Spalding sugar factory with a load of beet, this 1977 Southall built Marathon Mk II. The TL12 engine performed well in these vehicles, with very high mileages being recorded before overhaul became necessary. (*Bill Taylor*)

Right: The long wheel base rigid version of the Marathon was not very common, and this TL12 engined Mk I, with a draw bar trailer was owned by a straw merchant from Crowle, near Scunthorpe. It was seen at Ferrybridge Services on 16th August 1989, then almost 14 years old. (*Author*)

Bottom left: When this photograph was first discovered, no details of the tractor unit were known, and it was assumed that it was probably a prototype connected with the FPT 70 premium truck project. However, further research has uncovered detailed chassis and cab interior photographs which suggests that it was something entirely separate from the Marathon project. It is V8 powered with chassis number 3VTG6R9AE 090 Mk I. No other AEC V8 chassis had the 3VTG prefix. It has twin air cleaners and exhaust stacks, no clutch pedal, with a semi-automatic gearbox, double drive Leyland Group hub reduction rear axles with cross-axle and inter-axle diff-locks, exhaust brake, and a comprehensive range of instruments and warning lights. These included 4 brake air pressure gauges, rev-counter, tachograph showing just 3.2 kilometres covered, time clock, engine oil level gauge, engine and gearbox oil pressure gauges, engine oil temperature gauge, ammeter, fuel gauge, and coolant temperature gauge. The right hand control cab has Bostrom Viking seats for the driver and passenger. One wonders whatever became of this fascinating vehicle. (*AEC*)

APPENDIX I

AEC DIESEL ENGINES

ENGINE TYPE	CAPACITY* (Approx)	CYLIN-DERS	BORE & STROKE mm	COMBUSTION CHAMBER	LINER TYPE	FIRING ORDER	POWER RATING bhp	APPLICATION
A165	8.81	6	115x142	Comet Mk 1	Dry	153624	120	Goods and Passenger
A166	5.51	4	108x146	Comet Mk 1	Dry	1342	75	Goods and Passenger
A168	6.61	4	120x146	Comet Mk 1	Dry	1342	85	Goods and Passenger
A170	7.71	6	105x146	Comet Mk 1	Dry	153624	115	Q Bus, anti-clockwise
A170DI	7.71	6	105x146	Direct Inj.	Dry	153624	95-105	Passenger
A171	7.71	6	105x146	Comet Mk 1	Dry	142635	115	Goods and Passenger
A172	6.61	6	105x130	Comet Mk 2	Wet	153624	100	Passenger
A173	7.71	6	105x146	Direct Inj.	Dry	142635	95	Goods and Passenger
A175	8.81	6	115x142	Comet Mk 3	Dry	153624	100	Marine
A176	5.51	4	108x146	Comet Mk 1	Dry	1342	100	Marine and Marine auxiliary
A177	8.81	6	115x142	Comet Mk 3	Dry	153624	100	Marine auxiliary
A178	8.81	6	115x142	Comet Mk 3	Dry	153624	100	Industrial
A180	8.81	6	115x142	Direct Inj.	Dry	153624	115	Goods and Passenger
A183	6.61	6	105x130	Comet Mk 3	Wet	153624	100	L.H. Matilda Tank
A184	6.61	6	105x130	Comet Mk 3	Wet	153624	100	R.H. Matilda Tank
A186	6.61	4	120x146	Direct Inj.	Dry	1342	85	Goods and Passenger
A187	7.71	6	105x146	Direct Inj.	Dry	142635	105	0853 Matador, 0854 6x6
A190	9.61	6	120x142	Comet Mk 3	Dry	153624	145	Valentine Tank
A195	7.71	6	105x146	Direct Inj.	Dry	142635	105	Armoured Car Mk 1
A196	7.71	6	105x146	Direct Inj.	Dry	142635	105	W.D. Petrol Tanker
A197	9.61	6	120x142	Comet Mk 3	Dry	153624	145	Armoured Car Mk 2 and 3
A198	9.61	6	120x142	Comet Mk 3	Dry	153624	145	Armoured Command Vehicle 6x6
A200	9.61	6	120x142	Comet Mk 3	Dry	153624	100	War Dept. Whale Generator
A202	7.71	6	105x146	Direct Inj.	Dry	142635	95	Gardner 5LW replacement
A204	9.61	6	120x142	Direct Inj.	Dry	153624	105	London Transport only
A205	9.61	6	120x142	Direct Inj.	Dry	153624	125	Oilfield Tractor 6x6
A206	9.61	6	120x142	Direct Inj.	Dry	153624	125	0366/20, 0386/20 Mammoth Major
A207	9.61	6	120x142	Direct Inj.	Dry	153624	125	Passenger, L.H. control
A208	9.61	6	120x142	Direct Inj.	Dry	153624	125	Passenger, Fluid transmission
A209	9.61	6	120x142	Comet Mk 3	Dry	153624	120	Starboard Marine, clockwise
A210	9.61	6	120x142	Comet Mk 3	Dry	142635	120	Port Marine, anti-clockwise
A211	9.61	6	120x142	Comet Mk 3	Dry	153624	100	Industrial
A212	9.61	6	120x142	Direct Inj.	Dry	153624	100	Marine auxiliary
A213	9.61	6	120x142	Direct Inj.	Dry	153624	125	Passenger, Crash gearbox
A214	11.31	6	130x142	Direct Inj.	Dry	153624	120	Blaw-Knox
A215	9.61	6	120x142	Direct Inj.	Dry	153624	120	Railcar
A216	9.61	6	120x142	Direct Inj.	Dry	153624	125	Goods Mk III range
A217	9.61	6	120x142	Direct Inj.	Dry	153624	125	Goods and Passenger L.H. control
A218	9.61	6	120x142	Direct Inj.	Dry	153624	125	Passenger
A219	9.61	6	120x142	Direct Inj.	Dry	153624	125	Passenger, underfloor
A220	11.31	6	130x142	Direct Inj.	Dry	153624	159	Railcar turbo-charged
A221	11.31	6	130x142	Direct Inj.	Dry	153624	140	Goods and Passenger
A222	11.31	6	130x142	Direct Inj.	Dry	153624	140	Goods and Passenger L.H. control
A223	11.31	6	130x142	Direct Inj.	Dry	153624	140	Militant Mk I
A224	9.61	6	120x142	Direct Inj.	Dry	153624	100	Industrial
A225	9.61	6	120x142	Direct Inj.	Dry	153624	100	Industrial with clutch and P.T.O.
A226	11.31	6	130x142	Direct Inj.	Dry	153624	130	Industrial
A227	11.31	6	130x142	Direct Inj.	Dry	153624	130	Industrial with clutch and P.T.O.
A230	11.31	6	130x142	Direct Inj.	Dry	153624	140	Railcar Vertical
AV275	275 cu.in.	4	105x130	Direct Inj.	Wet	1342	65-75	Goods (non-AEC)

ENGINE TYPE	CAPACITY* (Approx)	CYLIN-DERS	BORE & STROKE mm	COMBUSTION CHAMBER	LINER TYPE	FIRING ORDER	POWER RATING bhp	APPLICATION
AV275G	275 cu.in.	4	105x130	Direct Inj.	Wet	1342	64-73	Industrial
AV312	312 cu.in.	4	112x130	Direct Inj.	Wet	1342	75-85	Goods (non-AEC)
AV312G	312 cu.in.	4	112x130	Direct Inj.	Wet	1342	60-75	Industrial
AV/AH410	410 cu.in.	6	105x130	Direct Inj.	Wet	153624	102-128	Goods and Passenger
AV410G	410 cu.in.	6	105x130	Direct Inj.	Wet	153624	80-102	Industrial
AV/AH470	470 cu.in.	6	112x130	Direct Inj	Wet	153624	115-144	Goods and Passenger
AV470G	470 cu.in.	6	112x130	Direct Inj.	Wet	153624	90-112	Industrial
AVT470/AHT470	470 cu.in.	6	112x130	Direct Inj.	Wet	153624	155-171	Goods and Passenger, export Turbo-charged
AVT470G	470 cu.in.	6	112x130	Direct Inj.	Wet	153624	150-171	Industrial Turbo-charged
AV/AH590	590 cu.in.	6	120x142	Direct Inj.	Wet	153624	125-159	Goods and Passenger
AV590G	590 cu.in.	6	120x142	Direct Inj.	Wet	153624	125-150	Industrial
AV/AH690	690 cu.in.	6	130x142	Direct Inj.	Wet	153624	150-192	Goods and Passenger
AV690G	690 cu.in.	6	130x142	Direct Inj.	Wet	153624	150-192	Industrial
AVT690/AHT690	690 cu.in.	6	130x142	Direct Inj.	Wet	153624	230-250	Goods and Passenger export Turbo-charged
AVT690G	690 cu.in.	6	130x142	Direct Inj.	Wet	153624	220-250	Industrial, Turbo-charged
AV1100	1100 cu.in.	6	156x156	Direct Inj.	Wet	153624	175-300	Specialised Goods, Industrial
AH1100	1100 cu.in.	6	156x156	Direct Inj.	Wet	153624	275-300	Railcar
AVT1100	1100 cu.in.	6	156x156	Direct Inj.	Wet	153624	300-385	Turbo-charged, 18 cu.yd.DK4
AHT1100	1100 cu.in.	6	156x156	Direct Inj.	Wet	153624	360-400	Railcar
AV/AH471	471 cu.in.	6	112x130	Direct Inj.	Dry	153624	115-135	Goods, Passenger, Industrial
AV/AH505	505 cu.in.	6	116x130	Direct Inj.	Dry	153624	135-182	Goods, Passenger, Industrial
AV/AH506	505 cu.in.	6	116x130	Direct Inj.	Dry	153624	130-150	Goods, Passenger (in-line pump)
AV691	690 cu.in.	6	130x142	Direct Inj.	Dry	153624	192-206	Goods, Passenger, Industrial
AH691	690 cu.in.	6	130x142	Direct Inj.	Dry	153624	180-206	Passenger
AV760	760 cu.in.	6	136x142	Direct Inj.	Dry	153624	180-265	Goods, Industrial
AH760	760 cu.in.	6	136x142	Direct Inj.	Dry	153624	160-220	Passenger
V8-800	740 cu.in.	8	130x114	Direct Inj.	Dry	15486372	225-247	Goods, Passenger,Industrial
V8-801	800 cu.in.	8	135x114	Direct Inj.	Dry	15486372	240-275	Goods, Industrial
TL12	760 cu.in.	6	136x142	Direct Inj.	Dry	153624	265-280	Goods
L12	760 cu.in.	6	136x142	Direct Inj.	Dry	153624	210-230	Goods

NOTES

1. *Denotes the approximate engine capacities and refers to the designation by which the engines were commonly known and refered to. Actual capacities for the engines relevant to the lorries described in this book are:-

ENGINE	CAPACITY (LITRES)	ENGINE	CAPACITY (LITRES)
7.7 -	7.581	A690/691	11.310
9.6	9.630	A1100	17.892
11.3	11.300	A505/506	8.226
A410	6.754	A760/TL12/L12	12.473
A470/471	7.685	V8-800	12.154
A590	9.640	V8-801	13.100

2. All engine power outputs are quoted in metric horsepower, corrected to 29.92 ins. Hg and 60°F conditions.
3. AEC fitted a variety of fuel pump equipment to their direct injection engines through the years, including both inline and distributor type pumps manufactured by Simms, CAV, and Bosch.
4. The above list does not include experimental engines, and certain other types which were manufactured for London Transport; for instance there was an A185 9.6 litre unit fitted to very early Regent Mk III RTs, which was a bored out version of the 8.8 litre, but this was not the same as the A206 9.6 litre engine used in the post-war Mk II and Mk III ranges, (See Chapter One). It has frequently been written that this engine was derived from the 8.8 litre, but it was a totally different design.

APPENDIX II

AEC LORRY RANGE FROM 1934

All models listed are Forward Control, unless stated otherwise. Most were available with either right or left hand control. The years of manufacture are approximate, as often, new types were announced at the Commercial Motor Show, but volume production would not commence until the following year. When a model was superceded, there was often a considerable period of overlap with its successor.

MODEL NUMBER	NAME	YEAR
344	Monarch Mk I, 4 cyl. engine	1934-40
0244	Monarch Mk II, normal control, 4 cyl.	1935-40
0266	Mammoth Major Six Mk II, normal Control	1934-36
0346	*Monarch/Matador Mk II, 6 cyl. engine	1935-40
0246	Matador Mk II, normal control, 6 cyl.	1935-40
0366	Mammoth Major Six Mk II	1935-40
0386	Mammoth Major Eight Mk II	1935-40
0366L	Mammoth Minor	1937-41
853	War Dept. 4x4 Matador tractor, (petrol)	1939-45
854	War Dept. 6x6 Petrol Tanker, (petrol)	1940-45
0853	War Dept. 4x4 Matador tractor, diesel	1939-45,1953-59
0854	War Dept. 6x6 Petrol Tanker, diesel	1940-44
0855	Armoured Car Mk I	1942
0856	Armoured Car Mk II and III	1943-44
0857	6x6 Armoured Command Vehicle	1944-45
0858	6x6 Oilfield tractor, normal control	1946-48
0346S	Monarch Mk II	1945-47
0347	Matador Mk II (4x2)	1945-47
0366/20	Mammoth Major Six Mk II	1945-48
0386/20	Mammoth Major Eight Mk II	1945-48
0248	Special chassis, bonneted, L.H. control	1945-47
3451	Monarch Mk III	1947-56
3471	Matador Mk III (4x2)	1947-50
2481	Matador Mk III normal control, export	1947-48
2482,3	Matador Mk III normal control, export	1948-57
3671,2,3	Mammoth Major Six Mk III	1948-60
2671	Mammoth Major Six Mk III, normal control	1948-61
3681,2,3	Mammoth Major Six Mk III	1949-61
2681	Mammoth Major Six Mk III, normal control	1949-62
3871,2,3	Mammoth Major Eight Mk III	1948-60
3881,2	Mammoth Major Eight Mk III	1948-61
3472.4.5	Mandator Mk III	1950-60
2472	Mandator Mk III normal control	1950-61
3481,2,3,4	Mandator Mk III	1950-62
3521	Majestic (twin steer)	1950-56
3531	Majestic (twin steer)	1951-57
0859	M.O.S. Militant 6x4 general purpose	1951-62
0860	M.O.S. Militant 6x6 recovery etc.	1951-62
GM4RA	Mercury Mk I, 12 tons G.V.W.	1953-61
2GM4RA	Mercury Mk II, 14 tons G.V.W.	1956-65
GM4LA, 2GM4LA	Monarch Mk V and VI export	1955-65
2421,31	Mammoth Mk III normal control	1956-62
2621,31,2,3	Mammoth Major Mk III normal control	1956-62
GM6RH	Mustang (twin steer)	1956-61
3673M	Dumptruk Mk III derived	1957-63
G4RA	Mandator Mk V	1958-66

MODEL NUMBER	NAME	YEAR
G6RA	Mammoth Major Six Mk V	1958-66
G8RA	Mammoth Major Eight Mk V	1958-66
GB4	Mogul normal control, (4x2)	1958-67
GB6	Majestic normal control, (6x4)	1958-68
M4RA,LA	Ranger bus, Mercury derived	1958-79
4GM4R,L	**Matador Mk II 4x4, AV470	1959-60
GM6RAS	Marshal (6x2)	1960-66
GM6RAT	Marshal (6x4)	1960-66
2SRA/4RA	Kudu bus, loosely Mandator based	1961-70
HG6RAB	Super Mammoth normal control	1961-65
DK6RAB	Dumptruk normal control	1961-62
DK4RA	Dumptruk AVT1100 normal control	1961-63
G6LA	Mammoth Major Six Mk V export	1963-66
G4LA	Mandator Mk V export	1963-66
HDK4R	AVT1100 Dumptruk normal control	1964-65
BDK6R	690 Dumptruk normal control	1964-71
TG4R	Mandator AV691/760	1965-77
TGM4R	Mercury AV471/505/506	1965-77
TGM6R	Marshal AV505/506	1966-77
TG6R	Mammoth Major Six AV691/760	1966-77
TG8R	Mammoth Major Eight AV691/760	1966-77
TG6RF	Mammoth Minor AV691/760 twin steer	1965-70
4G6R4B	***Mammoth Major Six Special Tipper	1966-74
0870,0880	Militant Mk III, R.H./L.H. control	1966-71
VTG4R	Mandator V8	1968-69
TGM8R	Marshal Eight AV505	1968-70
2VTG6R	Mammoth Major Six V8 tractor unit	1969
2TG6R	Marshal Major AV760	1971-76
2T25/27	Marathon Mk 1 and 2	1973-79

NOTES

1. *Similar specification, except that the Matador version was equipped for drawbar trailer operations.
2. As the Mercury, Mk V, and tilt-cab ranges progressed they were prefixed with a single number to denote detail improvements or changes in specification, e.g. 2G6RA, 5TGM4R etc.
3. ** Only 43 of these were produced for home and overseas markets. A 4x4 version of the Mandator Mk V was also produced in prototype form, aimed at a specialist tipper market in mountainous regions of Europe.
4   ***Available with a fixed cab, either Mk V style, or proprietary Motor Panels one, as fitted to contemporary Seddon and Guy.